Diesels on the London Midland

MICHAEL WELCH

Rails

Published by Rails Publishing

Printed by Parksons Graphics

Layout by Michael Welch. Typesetting and book production by Lucy Frontani.

Front Cover: Bathed in glorious spring sunshine on 18th May 1978, Class 45 No.45 019 powering the 11.50am Glasgow Central to Nottingham has just emerged from Birkett tunnel and is heading towards Ais Gill summit on the legendary Settle & Carlisle line. *Chris Evans*

Back cover: Perhaps the best-loved class featured in this book, the English Electric Type 4 1Co-Co1 locomotives were an integral part of operations on the London Midland Region for many years. In this illustration the distant Lake District fells provide the backdrop as No.D314 heads southwards near Milnthorpe on 11th April 1968. By the date of this picture BR's corporate blue and grey livery was becoming increasingly common up and down the network, but No.D314 had yet to be repainted and still looked reasonably presentable in traditional green and, many folk would argue, much more attractive as a result. *Tommy Tomalin*

Title page: The distinctive platform canopies and nearby office buildings provide a clue to the location of this shot – yes, its Manchester's Oxford Road station. A 2-car Derby-built unit is seen awaiting departure with a train to Warrington Central on 8th April 1973. Note that the unit's cyclic diagram information is displayed in the cab window, in this case indicating that it was based at Allerton and working diagram number 272. *Terry Philips*

Details of Michael Welch's other railway titles can be found at www.capitaltransport.com

Introduction

When asked to explain the link that Sheffield, Swindon, Stockport and Stockton-on-Tees have with BR's 1955 Modernisation Plan most railway enthusiasts will probably be completely baffled and probably shake their heads in disbelief when told that they are all locations where rolling stock was constructed. In fact, those diverse places were all involved with providing locomotives and rolling stock for use on the London Midland Region and this illustrates the incredible variety of designs that could be seen on that Region's territory.

The 'Big Four' companies had made the first tentative steps towards dieselisation prior to the Second World War building railcars and diesel shunters of various shapes and sizes but the outbreak of hostilities in 1939 put further development on the back burner. In 1947 the London Midland & Scottish Railway (LMSR), in association with English Electric, led the way with the production of the very first main line diesel locomotive to be produced in Great Britain, No.10000, and this was put through its paces on its first official run between Euston and Watford on 18th December 1947. No.10000, which bore a striking resemblance to locomotives being produced in North America at that time, later commenced regular operation in tandem with its sister engine, No.10001, on the crack 'Royal Scot' express. When BR's much vaunted Modernisation Plan was announced in 1955, however, there were only seven main line diesel locomotives in use. A major development in the early 1950s was the construction of the Associated Commercial Vehicles/British United Traction Co. experimental lightweight diesel units which underwent trials on the Harrow & Wealdstone to Belmont branch. Undoubtedly, during this period much more progress was made with the introduction of railcars than locomotives and this culminated in the very first conversion of a steam operated local service, this being the Leeds to Bradford service that went over to DMU operation on 14th June 1954; a new maintenance depot, designed solely for diesel traction, was opened at Bradford (Hammerton Street). The new units had been designed and constructed at Derby and their attractive styling and passengers' unobstructed view of the line ahead were probably seen as revolutionary features at the time. The popularity of the DMUs, which offered a much cleaner and faster journey, was such that their use rapidly spread across the length and breadth of Great Britain and construction continued until 1963 when the Swindon 'Inter City' units, later known as Class 123, were introduced. BR workshops played their part in the construction of DMUs, notably Derby which turned out almost 1,400 vehicles, while many private builders produced a multiplicity of designs. Perhaps the best-known independent manufacturer was Metropolitan Cammell whose Washwood Heath, Birmingham, factory produced 760 cars altogether to their distinctive design and these gained a mention in the annals of railway history when in 2003 they were the very last fleet of 'first generation' units to be taken out of traffic. It was, perhaps, appropriate that the units were based at Longsight depot in Manchester that many years previously had been the last major city to witness regular steam operation.

The production of diesel locomotives proceeded more slowly – it should be remembered that BR was still building steam engines at that time – and it was June 1957 before the first machine rolled off the production line. This was No.D8000, a 1,000hp English Electric Type 1 (later Class 20) and was based at Great Britain's first mainland depot adapted to service main line diesel locomotives at Bow in East London. This machine had been built as part of the so-called 'pilot scheme' for the introduction of main line diesel traction which envisaged the building of 174 locomotives in various power bands to enable their performance to be evaluated and operating problems identified before large orders were placed. A few months later No.D5500, the first of the Brush Type 2 locomotives (later Class 31) entered traffic and other classes soon followed. This sensible and considered approach to dieselisation was soon blown off course, however, because a review of progress was taking place behind the scenes against a disturbing background of increasing road and air competition which was having a major impact on BR's traffic and finances. It was felt that the pace of change needed to be dramatically quickened in view of the loss of traffic and additional orders were placed for supposedly 'pilot scheme' locomotive types and, even worse, completely untried and untested designs were ordered straight from the drawing board, an ill advised decision that BR and its passengers certainly lived to regret during the ensuing years. In mid-May 1960 the British Transport Commission confirmed rumours filtering out from manufacturers and 'other sources' that BR had embarked on drastic action, a headlong rush to dieselise, this being seen as the only way that costs could be reduced, train services speeded up and the railway industry safeguarded. It was reported at this time that the number of locomotives on order had jumped from 174 to 1,653 and it was rumoured that political interference had resulted in BR placing orders with outside manufacturers whose world-wide reputation had been built up purely on their undisputed skill and experience in the construction of steam locomotives! Incredibly, in May 1960 no fewer than eleven outside contractors were involved in the building of diesel locomotives in addition to six BR workshops. The hasty and apparently uncoordinated placing of orders with so many different contractors resulted in a number of designs that were a complete liability once they entered traffic, and some classes were reportedly based at depots close to the original maker's works so they could be quickly returned for rectification when they failed in service. Outside manufacturers were not immune from the fallout from this situation, a notable casualty being the world-renowned North British Locomotive Co. which went into receivership in early 1962.

The LMR arguably fared better than other regions, generally using 2,000hp English Electric Type 4s on the West Coast Main Line and BR/Sulzer Type 4s on the former Midland lines and north-east to south-west route. The limitations of the former, which were under-powered for the heavy trains they worked, were masked by inflated schedules due to electrification work and, in any case, most were displaced by electric traction in 1966. The unreliable train heating boilers were frequently the Achilles heel of these types and their shortcomings certainly hit the headlines of the national press during the bitterly cold 1962/63 winter when many passengers endured long journeys in unheated trains. The worst performing locomotives on the LMR were the ill-fated Metrovick Co-Bos which spent long periods in store and defied all attempts to improve their reliability. They were banished to Barrow-in-Furness shed for duties on the relatively remote former Furness Railway lines but in the late 1960s the LMR's patience finally ran out and they were unceremoniously withdrawn.

In this album I have attempted to illustrate all of the first generation diesel locomotive and DMU classes that worked on the LMR, or on former LMR territory, during a 30-year period from the late 1950s. I have endeavoured to produce a balanced selection of photographs within the constraints of the available material. Inevitably some classes, such as the much-loved English Electric Type 4s, predominate whilst other types, that were perhaps not as numerous on the LMR, are not so well represented.

Compilation of this book has been enormously enjoyable and satisfying, and heartfelt thanks are offered to all of the photographers who kindly made their precious slides available for a wider audience to savour. In addition, thanks are also due to Chris Evans, Bob Dalton, Dave Fakes, Ron Herbert and Terry Phillips who have painstakingly read through the proof, corrected many inaccuracies and suggested numerous improvements and I am confident that a much better book has resulted.

Michael Welch
Burgess Hill,
West Sussex,
March 2017

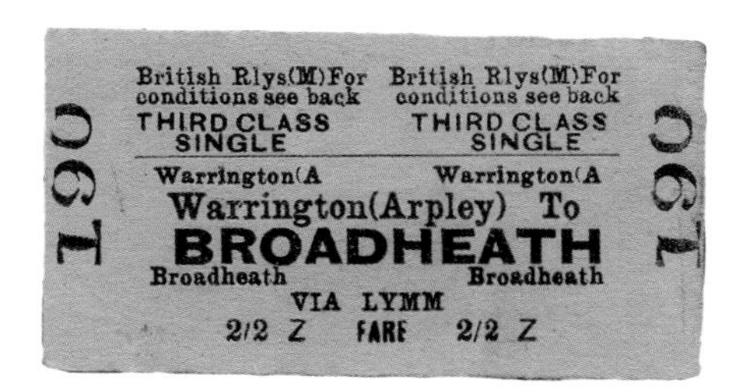

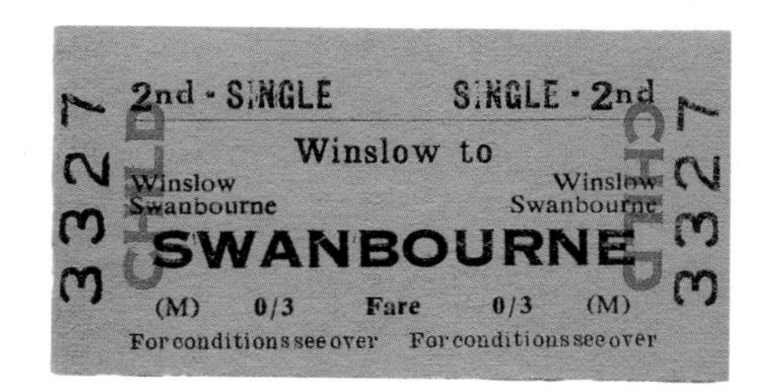

Contents

Flaming June at Crewe. The LMS was keen to extend the use of diesel traction and in early 1947 announced plans to operate main line locomotives rather than just shunting locomotives that were already in use throughout its system. The first main line diesel locomotive to be built in Great Britain was No.10000 which was constructed by the LMS at Derby works in association with English Electric, the project being under the direction of H.G. Ivatt. No.10000 weighed 127 tons, was fitted with a 1,600hp 16SVT engine which powered six traction motors and had a top speed of 93mph; the locomotive was finished in black livery with chromatic silver lining. On 18th December 1947 No.10000 was unveiled to the press and made a short run from Euston to Watford and back to show its capabilities. A sister locomotive, No.10001, emerged from Derby works in July 1948 but by that time the railway network had been nationalised and that machine had been built under BR jurisdiction, but its conception and design, like that of No.10000, had been undertaken entirely by the LMS. No.10000 was used on services between London St. Pancras and Derby in early 1948 and also made sorties to Manchester Central. During the early 1950s both machines were regularly used in tandem on the 'Royal Scot' between Euston and Glasgow and the 'Red Rose' from Euston to Liverpool. Between March 1953 and early 1955 they were based on the Southern Region working the prestigious 'Bournemouth Belle' and they also made occasional trips to Exeter. They later returned to their old haunts on the LMR and could be found hauling the 'Royal Scot' and other expresses on that route. They lost their black livery during visits to Derby works for overhaul, emerging in standard green livery with the appropriate orange and black lining. The introduction of pilot scheme locomotives in the late 1950s caused a decline in their activities and No.10000 was eventually withdrawn in December 1963 after a relatively short life but, being the first main line diesel locomotive ever produced in Great Britain, at least it had an assured place in the annals of railway history. Its sister locomotive No.10001 remained in traffic on sporadic low profile goods duties until it, too, was withdrawn in March 1966. Here, Nos.10001 and 10000, hauling the down 'Royal Scot', are seen brightening up an otherwise dismal day at Crewe. Note the crew member in the cab of the second locomotive indicating that the locomotives were being operated in tandem; this picture was taken on 30th June 1957. *Colour Rail.com*

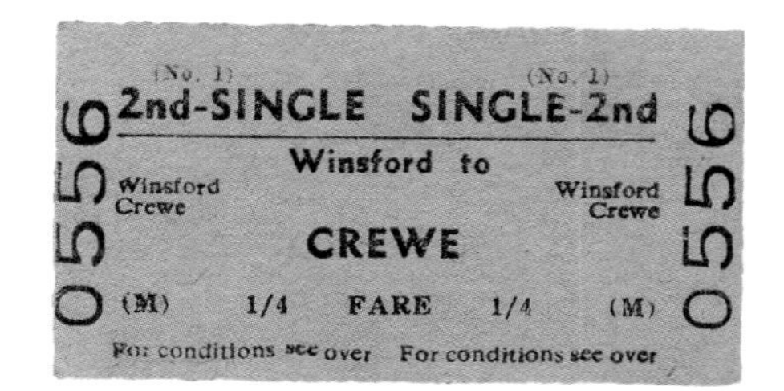

One of the aspects of railways that made the hobby so fascinating was the remarkable array of motive power still to be seen on the system in the early 1960s as the replacement of steam traction got underway. English Electric Type 4 locomotives weighing 133 tons had just been introduced but here is a diminutive locomotive at the other end of the scale – the complete opposite. No.ED1 may not look impressive but at least it could claim to be one of a select band of pre-nationalisation diesel locomotives, even if it was not a 'trailblazer'. Built by John Fowler & Co. in 1936, this 25-ton machine had a six cylinder Ruston & Hornsby engine which produced 88hp. It appears to have been the smallest of a number of diesel shunters constructed by that firm prior to the Second World War, Nos. ED2 to ED6 all being considerably more powerful. No.ED1 was numbered in the departmental series and appears to have spent its entire career at Beeston creosote works where other service locomotives were also employed. When this picture was taken at Derby works on 1st April 1962 No.ED1's mundane existence at nearby Beeston had ended and it was awaiting breaking-up. *R.C. Riley collection*

Compilation of an album of this type is dependent upon the goodwill of many photographers but there are always locomotive classes that prove hard to find and undoubtedly pictures of diesel shunters have presented a problem, an author's occupational hazard one might say. Among the most elusive have been photographs of the early LMS 0-6-0 diesel shunting locomotives with their unusual jackshaft drive. These locomotives, which weighed 54 tons 16 cwt., were powered by an English Electric 6-cylinder 350hp engine which provided power to a single motor. A total of 40 of these machines was built by the LMS at Derby works between May 1939 and June 1942, of which ten were requisitioned by the War Department and later saw service in Egypt; the remainder were taken into BR stock upon nationalisation and numbered 12003 to 12032. In this picture No.12014 is depicted shunting at Garston, Liverpool, on 23rd October 1963. This particular locomotive was constructed in March 1940 and was initially based at Toton as LMS No.7091, but when this shot was taken it was allocated to Speke Junction shed. The last of these locomotives was withdrawn from service *en masse* in December 1967. *G.D. Smith/Online Transport Archive*

Introduced in October 1952 when No.13000 was released from Derby works, BR's 350hp diesel shunters were destined to range far and wide across the network and became so commonplace in yards and depots they often went unnoticed. The design, which was largely based on an LMS class introduced in 1945, generally employed a six-cylinder 350hp English Electric engine which powered two nose-suspended traction motors. Construction continued until late 1962 and during this ten-year period examples were built at Crewe, Darlington, Derby, Doncaster and Horwich works. Some members of the class were withdrawn in the 1960s but mass condemnations did not commence until the 1970s when the contraction of BR's wagonload freight business resulted in the closure of many goods depots thus considerably reducing shunting requirements. In this picture D3052, one of the early members of the class dating from May 1954, is seen shunting empty coaches at Euston on 3rd September 1970. The locomotive is in deplorable external condition but at least its original BR totem and old style cab numerals can be easily discerned despite its thick covering of grime. No.D3052 was destined to remain in traffic until December 1973 and later made what was probably its longest ever journey *en route* to Cashmore's scrap yard at Newport in South Wales for breaking-up. *Terry Phillips*

Another view taken at Garston, this time on 5th May 1967, showing diesel mechanical 0-6-0 shunting engine No.D2553 apparently taking a long line of mineral wagons to the docks. This was one of 69 identical locomotives, Nos. D2550 to D2618, constructed by the Hunslet Engine Co. between October 1955 and March 1961. These 204hp machines weighed 30 tons (with variations) and were fitted with a Gardner type 8L3 engine. No.D2553 (formerly No.11139) dated from February 1956 and was originally based at Norwich (Thorpe) shed but was eventually withdrawn from Speke Junction depot in January 1968. Several have been preserved.
E.V. Richards/Online Transport Archive

The 350hp shunters were equally at home working at busy city termini, as seen in a previous picture, or at comparatively remote industrial installations. This picture was taken near a cement works at Hope in Derbyshire on 5th May 1981 and depicts No.08 879 approaching the junction with the main Manchester to Sheffield line. This route was considered for closure during the Beeching era due to the high cost of maintaining Cowburn and Totley tunnels, both of which are among the longest in Great Britain, and the rival Woodhead line was then the preferred route between Manchester and Sheffield. However, in a complete reversal of fortunes, the Woodhead route was eventually closed while the Hope Valley line survived and is now the sole route connecting those cities. No. 08 879 was one of a large batch of these machines constructed at Darlington works and entered service in January 1961 as D4047 at Sheffield (Grimethorpe) shed. *Tommy Tomalin*

In the early 1960s BR had a bewildering selection of small diesel shunters of various shapes and sizes on its books, among them No.D2864 which was photographed at Newton Heath shed on 5th April 1970, having been withdrawn from service just a few weeks previously. Sister locomotive No.D2869 is also visible; that locomotive was also out of use, having been withdrawn in December 1969. No.D2864 was a member of one of the smaller classes, of which 20 examples were constructed by the Yorkshire Engine Company in 1960/61. These machines were powered by a 170hp Rolls Royce engine, had hydraulic transmission and weighed 28 tons. They may not have been the most powerful, or impressive, diesel shunter on BR's books at the time but they were probably one of the most nimble, being designed for use in goods yards or on the dockside where all but the smallest locomotives were prohibited due to exceptionally tight curves. The class will probably be most associated with Liverpool docks, almost half of the class being based at Bank Hall shed, but a small batch was also allocated to Fleetwood. A few locomotives lasted long enough in traffic to be classified 02 under TOPS. *Rail Photoprints*

In 1949 the frames for a new 1Co-Co1 diesel locomotive, No.10201, were laid at Ashford works and it eventually entered traffic in November 1950; this locomotive was fitted with an English Electric 16-cylinder engine which developed 1,750hp and powered six traction motors. No.10201 was displayed at the Festival of Britain celebrations in May 1951 where its striking black livery with silver lining no doubt created quite a stir. A second, identical locomotive, No.10202, was completed and went into service in August 1951. In March 1954 a third locomotive in the series, No.10203, took to the rails but this was slightly more powerful and boasted an output of 2,000hp; this machine, which was constructed at Brighton, was regarded as 7P/6F in the steam locomotive classification system. O.V.S. Bulleid, Chief Mechanical Engineer of the Southern Railway, had been involved with the design and all three locomotives were built to the same profile as Bulleid's loco-hauled coaching stock. No.10203 was based at Nine Elms for its first year in service and undertook duties on the Waterloo to Exeter route; its sister locomotives, and LMS-designed Nos.10000 and 10001, were also allocated to that shed during this period. In July 1955 No.10203 was transferred to the LMR and based at Camden, working along the WCML to Manchester, Carlisle and Glasgow in addition to powering Euston to Bletchley local trains. No.10203 was later overhauled at Derby works who repainted it in standard green livery with the usual lining. Towards the end of the 1950s the locomotive, together with Nos.10201 and 10202, was spending a lot of time idle as new diesels started to come on stream and its inevitable withdrawal occurred in December 1963. Regrettably, none of these early main line diesel locomotives was preserved and all were cut up for scrap, after a protracted period of storage, at the yard of J. Cashmore, Great Bridge, in 1968. This portrait recalls the glory days of this locomotive which is seen powering the 'Royal Scot' at Weaver Junction in July 1958; note the prominent position of the headboard. Strangely, three people are leaning out of carriage windows which suggests some sort of incident may have occurred – surely the locomotive had not broken down! *The late Roy Whitfield/Rail Photoprints*

Various dates in the more recent history of the railways stand out, such as 1st January 1948 when the system was nationalised and 18th April 1966 when full electric services commenced on the West Coast main line, but is unlikely that 14th June 1954 will resonate with many enthusiasts. This was the date when the very first conventional diesel multiple units (DMUs) were introduced between Leeds and Bradford. A three-car demonstration train had been built by Associated Commercial Vehicles in 1952 and this pioneer unit could operate as a one-, two-, or three-car formation by virtue of its multiple control system. The unit ran trials in various parts of the country and a further eight cars were constructed, but the design was not perpetuated and the cars were withdrawn in 1959. The units used between Leeds and Bradford were 'Derby Lightweight' two-car sets powered by four Leyland 125hp engines, had hydraulic transmission and a control system that soon became non-standard. Both cars were powered due to the steep gradients on this section. The bodies were constructed wholly of alloy to save weight, and the availability of steel supplies was also a factor at the time. All DMUs were given a coupling code in order to distinguish cars that could run together and these early 'Derby Lightweight' sets were coded red triangle. Unfortunately, their unique control system precipitated their early withdrawal and all of the vehicles were condemned just prior to their tenth birthday. The West Cumberland lines were next in line for modernisation and the first of those, from Carlisle to Silloth, was dieselised from 29th November 1954 while the remaining services to Keswick and Whitehaven were turned over to DMU operation in early 1955. Those routes employed standard 'Derby Lightweight' units which were equipped with two 150hp engines rather than four fitted to the earlier units; they were coded yellow diamond, this being an early code used for units in the 79xxx series. The first batches of units had full height windscreens but strengthening bars were deemed necessary and later vehicles incorporated these from new. The Carlisle-based units were fitted with window bars due to the very restricted clearances on certain sections of the former Maryport & Carlisle line. Subsequently, 'Derby Lightweight' units appeared in many parts of the country but were particularly associated with secondary lines in East Anglia and Lincolnshire while a batch was based at Stratford shed, East London, for a time for use on the Romford to Upminster line and Southminster branch. In this picture a 'Derby Lightweight' unit can be seen leading a four-coach Barrow to Lancaster train at Arnside on 11th April 1968, so it was probably on familiar territory. The viaduct there carries the line across the estuary of the river Kent which is noted for its fast flowing tides, so it is to be hoped that the owner of the car parked on the sands was able to make a quick getaway at the appropriate time! *Tommy Tomalin*

The 'Derby Lightweight' units could be observed in various parts of Great Britain and in this photograph the 6.18pm Cambridge to Bletchley train is seen passing Aspley Guise station on 21st June 1966. For reasons unknown to the author this working stopped at all stations between Cambridge and Bedford St. John's but then ran on to Bletchley as a semi-fast service omitting various stations including Aspley Guise. The introduction of DMUs was one of BR's early success stories and they often sparked a remarkable increase in passenger numbers prompting BR to order 1,400 vehicles in December 1954 at a cost of £17.5 million before the official launch of the modernisation plan some months later. Unfortunately, the widespread introduction of DMUs coincided with rapidly increasing competition from road transport and, despite vastly increased patronage and reduced costs, the units failed to stave off closure of many lines. The Cambridge-Bletchley-Oxford route's passenger service was merely listed for 'modification' in the 1963 Beeching report but the entire route was apparently added to the list of lines proposed for complete closure by the London Midland Region. Despite its close proximity to London some sections were sanctioned for abandonment but the Bletchley to Bedford stretch was reprieved due to the hardship that closure would cause to passengers. Ironically, Aspley Guise station was actually tabled for closure in the Beeching Report but survived and remains in business at the time of writing. *Tommy Tomalin*

A long journey in a DMU may not be everybody's idea of the perfect start or finish to a day out by the seaside but, even so, they were employed on such duties despite their somewhat spartan accommodation. Here, vehicle No.M79681 is the leading carriage of a long formation seen heading away from Llandudno with an unidentified return excursion on 29th May 1966; it is likely that this working was *en route* to Liverpool or Manchester. Let us hope that the day trippers had a relaxing day out! No.M79681 was officially known as a driving trailer composite lavatory (DTCL) vehicle, the first-class seating being immediately behind the driving compartment. This coach offered 12 seats in the superior accommodation and 53 second class seats, weighed 21 tons and was among the last series to be built in 1956. It was withdrawn in July 1967 and broken-up in February 1968. It was officially paired with No.M79180, a driving motor brake second (DMBS) which remained in traffic until April 1969 and was cut-up in December 1971; this coach weighed 27 tons and provided seating for 52 second class passengers. Clearly the coaches had been split up at some stage, the motor coach surviving much longer in service; the unit was coded yellow diamond. *Tommy Tomalin*

'Any more for Bletchley – this is almost your last chance', could well have been the cry from the porter at Buckingham on 5th September 1964, the last day of passenger services from the town. Here, 'Derby Lightweight' single car No.M79900 is seen standing in Buckingham station prior to leaving at 11.18am for Bletchley via Verney Junction. This particular vehicle had two BUT (AEC) 150hp engines, weighed 27 tons and was fitted with seats for 61 passengers. The route north of Buckingham originally ran as far as Banbury (Merton Street) but that section was closed to passengers on 2nd January 1961. The weekday service on the truncated branch consisted of nine trains to and from Bletchley and there was even a morning 'rush hour' period at Buckingham with three services to Bletchley between 7.14am and 8.25am. Two double ended single cars, Nos. M79900/1, were constructed for use on the branch in the hope that they would reduce operating costs and attract more passengers. The local travellers doubtless hoped that the units would prove to be the line's salvation, costs were reduced by a third and receipts apparently jumped by around 400%, but despite a transformation in the line's finances the deficit could not be entirely eliminated and it was proposed for closure. The cars were constructed in 1956 and were originally built with luggage compartments of different sizes, No.M79900 had a smaller van than its sister car, but it was quickly decided that its van was too small and it underwent modification at Derby. Judging by the number of parcels being loaded in this shot there would not have been very much space left for the guard so the enlargement was more than justified. One end of each car was disfigured by two sets of unsightly pipes, the exhaust pipes, and those to facilitate filling of the radiator header tanks. Following withdrawal No.M79900 was acquired by the Railway Technical Centre, Derby, for conversion to a mobile laboratory, numbered RDB 975010 and bestowed with the name *Iris*.
Terry Phillips

A ‘Derby Lightweight’ single car, forming the 5.57pm Buckingham to Bletchley train, is lost in the landscape as it heads away from Buckingham on 29th June 1964. The car’s rather ugly exhaust pipes can just be discerned. Padbury was the only intermediate station on the branch which joined the Oxford to Cambridge line at Verney Junction. *Tommy Tomalin*

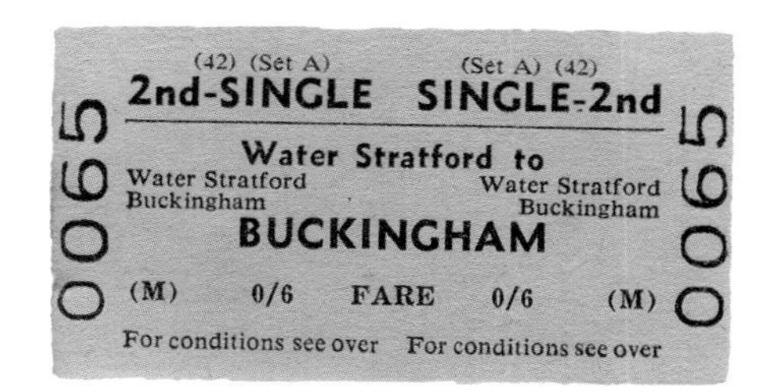

Power and speed personified. None of the experimental diesel locomotives produced by outside manufacturers could have had the dramatic impact of the prototype English Electric 'Deltic' when it took to the rails in October 1955. The considerable size of the locomotive, the distinctive noise of its engines and powder blue livery with aluminium embellishments must have created an immediate impression on train spotters and the general public at a time when the railway system was still almost totally reliant on steam traction. This striking 106 ton Co-Co locomotive, which was decorated with cream speed whiskers on each nose end, was powered by two Napier 'Deltic' 18-cylinder engines, each developing 1,650hp thus providing a total of 3,300hp through six axle-hung, nose-suspended traction motors. It was originally intended that it would be numbered DP1 (diesel prototype 1) but it never carried that number and was simply known as the 'Deltic' because, after all, it was unique. BR provided facilities for what were sometimes referred to as 'road tests' and the locomotive's first revenue-earning duties were on the West Coast Main Line where it was allocated to Edge Hill (Liverpool) shed for use on London express workings. In early 1959 it moved to the East Coast Main Line where it spent the first six months on clearance and performance tests, which included hauling mineral trains, before entering passenger service alongside brand new English Electric Type 4s and, of course, Gresley's celebrated Pacifics that were still in front-line service at that time. The 'Deltic' succumbed to a serious engine failure in March 1961 after amassing 450,000 miles in a relatively short period and the locomotive was banished to English Electric's Vulcan Foundry works at Newton-le-Willows in Lancashire. It had certainly created an impression! In 1963 the machine was presented to the Science Museum and later moved to the National Railway Museum at York. Here, the 'Deltic' is seen whisking the 'Merseyside Express' along at Halton Junction, south of Runcorn, on 4th August 1958. Note that the nose end was designed to incorporate a headlight, possibly with overseas orders in mind, but this was never fitted. *The late Roy Whitfield/Rail Photoprints*

A total of 760 Metropolitan-Cammell DMU cars was constructed at the company's Washwood Heath, Birmingham, works with the lion's share of 465 vehicles being allocated to the ER/NER, but all regions of BR, apart from the SR, eventually had an allocation. The modest number of units based on the WR was used on services on the cross-country line towards Redhill so units of this type actually worked on all regions – quite an achievement. The 'Met-Camm' units, as they were universally known, ran in two-, three- and four-car formations, 13 four-car sets being delivered to Darlington depot for services to Saltburn. During their lifetime the units were powered by a variety of engine types from various manufacturers including AEC and Leyland, the last-mentioned being the most common. These robust units were constructed with light alloy framework and roof panels, but the body ends were of steel to give strength and protection in the event of a collision. The DMBS coaches seated 52 second class passengers while the DTCL carriages provided space for 12 first and 53 second class passengers, but there were some variations. In the mid-1970s, with many units approaching their twentieth birthday, BR embarked on a massive refurbishment programme and a 'Met-Camm' unit, which by that time was known as Class 101, was selected as the prototype. Work was undertaken to minimise vibration from the engines, improve riding qualities, heating and lighting. This unit, sporting a brand-new livery, made a three-month tour of Great Britain to enable Passenger Transport Executives and other bodies interested in developing public transport to evaluate the improvements and comment on the new features. In the early 1990s it was becoming clear that a large number of units would be required for some years and a further scheme was launched to 'facelift' those with the longest life expectancy. This work was modest compared to the refurbishment programme but at least the appearance of the units was improved and, hopefully, welcomed by the travelling public. Apart from two single cars used by Chiltern Railways the Metropolitan-Cammell units were the final first generation DMUs to operate in Great Britain in ordinary traffic being based at Longsight, Manchester, depot from where they were withdrawn in late 2003. It was always great fun to sit behind the driver observing the 'road' ahead, an enjoyable experience sadly not possible with the Met-Camm's successors. In this illustration the 8.15am Holyhead to Crewe train, formed of a 2-car 'Met-Camm' plus a 2-car Derby-built unit, is depicted at Rhyl on 30th August 1965. In the background a lofty former London & North Western Railway signal box can be seen while partially visible behind it stands the former Rhyl motive power depot looking empty and forlorn.
Terry Phillips

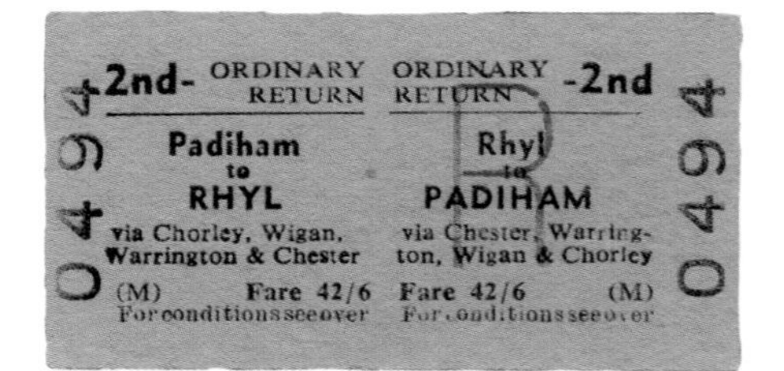

A bird's eye view of the attractive little station of Giggleswick which is located just west of Settle on the Leeds to Morecambe line. This picture, taken on 16th September 1967, features a Metropolitan-Cammell 2-car unit running-in with the 3.33pm Leeds to Morecambe Promenade train which was due to arrive at the Lancashire resort at 5.39pm – hardly a speedy journey for just over 60 miles. There were only half a dozen regular stopping trains each way on weekdays at that time but on Saturdays the line really came to life when many extra workings ran from the West Riding to Morecambe for the benefit of holiday-makers. The dull and misty weather conditions, so typical of this part of the world, do little to enhance the natural beauty of the fells in the distance. *Tommy Tomalin*

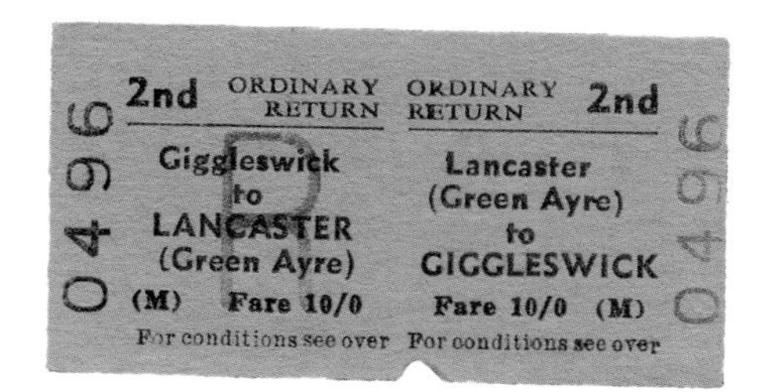

A Metropolitan-Cammell vehicle is the most prominent coach in this picture which was taken near Littleborough on 25th April 1968. It should be noted, however, that the unit is a hybrid and the other two coaches appear to be Gloucester R.C.W. vehicles. The identity of the train is not known but the photographer recorded that the shot was taken at 5.00pm so it is reasonable to assume it was the 4.05pm Leeds Central to Manchester Victoria. This is a really interesting location just a few hundred yards west of the entrance to Summit tunnel where just enough space has been found to build a cluster of mills and other buildings but the close proximity of the Pennine moors, which rise steeply on both sides of the valley, precluded any further development. Out of sight on the left of the photograph is the infant river Roch while also hidden from view, on the right, is the Rochdale canal. The architecture seen here is more reminiscent of Yorkshire and, indeed, the West Riding border was only a mile or so distant, passing over the top of Summit tunnel. *Tommy Tomalin*

The majority of Cravens-built units were 2-car sets but here is a picture of a 3-car Cravens DMU, forming the 1.20pm train from Peterborough East to Leicester London Road; it is seen at Melton Junction, just west of Melton Mowbray station, where the Nottingham line diverged from the Leicester route. This picture was taken on 20th August 1961. There were 19 three-car sets originally formed of a driving motor brake second (DMBS), trailer composite (TCL) and driving motor composite (DMCL) but no separate first class accommodation was apparently provided for non-smokers and the railway authorities were later obliged to convert part of the TCL vehicles for the use of non-smokers. The centre cars were withdrawn in the 1968-70 period thus converting the units to 2-car sets. The carriage nearest to the camera in this picture is a DMCL which was equipped with two 150hp engines and standard mechanical transmission. Cravens units were of all-steel construction, were generally powered by AEC engines, and closely resembled Mk.1 loco-hauled coaches because the same design of windows and doors was used. The DMBS coaches had 52 second class seats whereas the DTCL vehicles provided seats for 12 first and 51 second class passengers. An especially pleasing feature of most Cravens-built units was the unpainted driver's window frames but this unit has had its frames painted and the front end, which also lacks 'speed whiskers', looks rather uninspiring as a result. Despite the supposed drive towards standardisation on the railways in the 1950s/60s, there were regional variations with the two digit boxes, those on the LMR consisting of one piece of glass while units based on the ER and ScR apparently had two! A depot stores foreman's nightmare to be sure. The Cravens-built units were scheduled for early withdrawal and only a few allocated to the ScR were painted in blue/grey livery, most remaining in blue. An exception was a set comprised of vehicle Nos.53359 and 54122 which was repainted in green livery; its mandatory yellow panel had 'speed whiskers' added in black! Other units saw further use as parcels cars, sandite cars and route learning vehicles. The last units were withdrawn from passenger service in 1988. *Tommy Tomalin*

Manchester has the unenviable reputation of a city where it is always raining but here the sun is shining brightly as a 2-car Cravens DMU rolls into Moston station with the 2.54pm Rochdale to Manchester Victoria working on 31st August 1965. The unpainted aluminium driver's window frames will be noted but, like the rest of the unit, they seem to be in need of cleaning. Note that the platform on the right appears to be of wooden construction. Manchester is located in a valley and trains heading north-eastwards towards Rochdale are faced with a continuous climb, much of it at 1 in 150 or steeper, hence the prominent smoke marks on the bridge. *Terry Phillips*

Few rail journeys rival a trip along the Cumbrian coast line from Carnforth to Carlisle via Barrow-in-Furness and in times past it was possible to sit behind the driver of a DMU and really enjoy the view to the best advantage. In this splendid shot, taken on 27th July 1966, a Cravens 2-car unit is depicted running alongside the west bank of the river Kent estuary and approaching Kents Bank station with the 4.20pm Carnforth to Barrow working. The route between those stations is extremely circuitous with lovely coastal stretches and crosses the estuaries of the rivers Kent and Leven on two very long viaducts. Needless to say, the views of Morecambe Bay and the distant Lake District fells are memorable. This section of line has always been well patronised because the road between Carnforth and Barrow-in-Furness is forced to make a considerable detour inland, thus giving the railway a considerable advantage. *Tommy Tomalin*

The 4.40pm Skipton to Carlisle train is seen high up in the Pennines, between Garsdale and Ais Gill summit, on 11th May 1967; the train is about to enter Shotlock Hill tunnel. By the date of this photograph some cars had been repainted in the new corporate livery and in the case of most DMUs this was a rather drab all-over livery known officially as 'rail blue'. Initially, small yellow warning panels were applied, as seen here, but later full yellow ends became standard. The stopping passenger service between Skipton and Carlisle was extremely sparse because it served a scattered rural community with few large population centres. In 1967 the weekday service consisted of two return Skipton to Carlisle trains plus one or two odd short workings, mainly at the northern end of the route. *Tommy Tomalin*

Garston station, on the branch from Watford Junction to St. Albans Abbey, was opened on 7th February 1966 at a time when dozens of stations up and down Great Britain were being systematically closed as a result of the Beeching Plan for 'reshaping' the railway network, so Garston really bucked the trend. In this picture a Cravens DMU, forming the 1.23pm Watford to St. Albans on 26th March 1968, is seen leaving the station as a lady passenger makes her way to the exit. The unit is not carrying a tail lamp but a red marker light appears to be illuminated. *Terry Phillips*

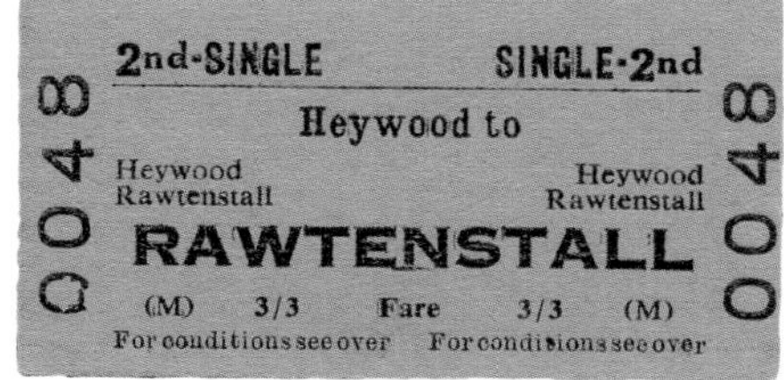

The image presented by BR to the travelling public was often not of the best and in this view of Rawtenstall station, taken on 22nd May 1968, the gas lighting and generally dilapidated state of the premises do little to welcome passengers. A Cravens unit is shown awaiting departure, forming the 10.05am train to Bury Bolton Street. Rawtenstall used to be a through station, as is evident from the picture, but the section beyond there to Bacup was closed to passenger traffic from 5th December 1966, this probably being the result of fierce competition from local buses which offered a more frequent, and doubtless cheaper, service. Later the surviving stub to Rawtenstall was also deprived of its passenger trains, this occurring on 5th June 1972. All was not lost at Rawtenstall, however, as the East Lancashire Railway subsequently took over the line to Bury and operates regular steam and diesel tourist trains. *Tommy Tomalin*

Few diesel classes produced under the modernisation plan were as successful as the English Electric Type 1 Bo-Bos, perhaps one of the most reliable and long-lived diesel locomotive designs of all time. The first example appeared in June 1957 and was allocated to Devons Road (Bow) shed in east London, BR's first depot solely for diesel locomotives, for employment on cross-London goods workings. The 1,000hp locomotives were constructed between 1957 and 1968 at the English Electric Co. (EE Co.) works at Newton-le-Willows, Lancashire, and Robert Stephenson & Hawthorns, Darlington, and were equipped with an EE Co. 8SVT engine. The locomotives, which weigh around 72 tons (with variations) have four axle-hung nose-suspended traction motors producing a tractive effort of 42,000lb. When the first machines came off the production lines in 1957 two other Type 1 designs, built by North British and British Thomson-Houston/Clayton, were being produced concurrently but both proved to be chronically unreliable, the former all being withdrawn in 1968 while a few of the latter soldiered on until March 1971 when they, too, went for scrap. In September 1962 the first Clayton Type 1s, with a centrally positioned full-width cab for better visibility, entered traffic and later the Western Region introduced its own hydraulic Type 1 design. Once again, both types were utter failures and the English Electric locomotives had been proved to be by far the most dependable and, while rival designs were coming and going at huge cost to the taxpayer, construction continued with the final locomotive, D8327, being out-shopped in February 1968. If any design had stood the all-important test of time this was surely it! Here, a brace of English Electric Type 1s, Nos.D8162 and D8061, disturb the peace of the Northamptonshire countryside near Lamport as they head towards Market Harborough with an empty coal train on 29th May 1969. *Tommy Tomalin*

Unglamorous workhorses. Here, a brace of English Electric Type 1s is seen at Coalville, on the Leicester to Burton-upon-Trent line, on 13th June 1970. The locomotives are Nos.D8118 and D8000 (yes, the prototype!) which are hauling a solitary brake van presumably after working a coal train. The latter locomotive remained in service until December 1980 and was rightly preserved as part of the National Collection; quite a few of these machines are still in service at the time of writing 60 years after the class's introduction. *Tommy Tomalin*

A pair of unidentified English Electric Type 1 Bo-Bos (later known as Class 20 under the TOPS scheme) approach Alfreton tunnel, between Trent and Chesterfield on the Erewash valley line, with a southbound goods working on 11th July 1970. The former station of Alfreton and South Normanton was closed to passenger traffic on 2nd January 1967 but reopened as Alfreton & Mansfield Parkway from 7th May 1973. This line ran through the heart of the Nottinghamshire coalfield and was a very busy freight artery, hence the four tracks to segregate passenger trains from slower moving goods workings. *Tommy Tomalin*

Many generations of railway enthusiasts flocked to classic photographic locations such as Ais Gill and Shap but Bagworth & Ellistown, alas, does not seem to have found favour with photographers. It was a station on the Leicester to Burton-upon-Trent line which lost its passenger trains from 7th September 1964 but stayed open for the very substantial mineral traffic produced by the collieries along the line and also a quarry at Bardon Mill. The station there was, in the best tradition of rural stations, located alongside a main road and both villages were about a mile distant, so it is inevitable that only the most determined and resourceful travellers ever used it. In this picture, taken north of the station on 22nd September 1970, the connection to Ellistown pit can be discerned just beyond the signal box, while a loaded coal train approaches behind Nos.8113 and 8065. On the left a line of empty wagons wait to be moved into the colliery complex for loading. It should be noted that by the date of this photograph the 'D' prefix to locomotive numbers had been abandoned. *Tommy Tomalin*

9668 **2nd-SINGLE SINGLE-2nd** 9668

Moira to

Moira Bagworth & Ellistown | Moira Bagworth & Ellistown

BAGWORTH & ELLISTOWN

(M) 1/10 Fare 1/10 (M)

For conditions see over | For conditions see over

The first 128 Class 20 locomotives constructed were fitted with disc indicators but the remainder had four-character headcode boxes as seen here on the front of No.20 173 photographed just west of Chinley station in Derbyshire on 29th May 1984; the other engine is sister locomotive No.20 163. Both locomotives were built by English Electric at Vulcan Foundry and entered service in late 1966. *Tommy Tomalin*

The Class 20s were, of course, built for freight haulage and not fitted with any form of train heating equipment which precluded their use on passenger services during the winter months, but during the summer there was no restriction and examples had a few booked diagrams on 'bucket and spade' seasonal trains. In this illustration a brace of Class 20s, Nos.20 140 and 20 160, are depicted arriving at Nottingham station with the 9.47am Derby to Skegness train on 1st August 1984 and the clear blue sky augurs well for a memorable, but perhaps bracing, day out on the Lincolnshire coast. In addition to day trippers, this train no doubt attracted local enthusiasts making the most of the opportunity to ride behind a pair of these distinctive locomotives. After all, there would not be much of a chance during the winter! *Tommy Tomalin*

Snowy conditions always add a different dimension to a photograph but falling snow, as seen here, is even better and full marks must be awarded to the hardy photographer whose fingers must have been extremely numb when he took this picture; the location is Tunstead, near Peak Forest, on the erstwhile Manchester Central to Derby main line. There is a massive limestone quarry at Peak Forest which produces a huge amount of traffic for the railway and in times past block trains made up of distinctive ICI hopper wagons ran between there and Northwich. Most sections of this route survived the Beeching era but, unfortunately, passenger services between Chinley and Matlock, a spectacular stretch of line, were withdrawn in July 1968 and the line's status as a traditional and very useful through route between Manchester and London was lost. South of Chinley the line continues to Peak Forest and, via a circuitous route, to Buxton; from there another line connects with one or two other quarries. In steam days enginemen always breathed a sigh of relief when Peak Forest was reached because it marked the summit of the old Midland route and it would be downhill virtually all of the way to either Derby or Manchester. Here, Class 20 No.20 159, accompanied by an unidentified sister locomotive, is seen heading north towards the 1mile 1,124yards-long Dove Holes tunnel and Chinley. The photographer even recorded one of the engine numbers – what a hero! *Rail Photoprints*

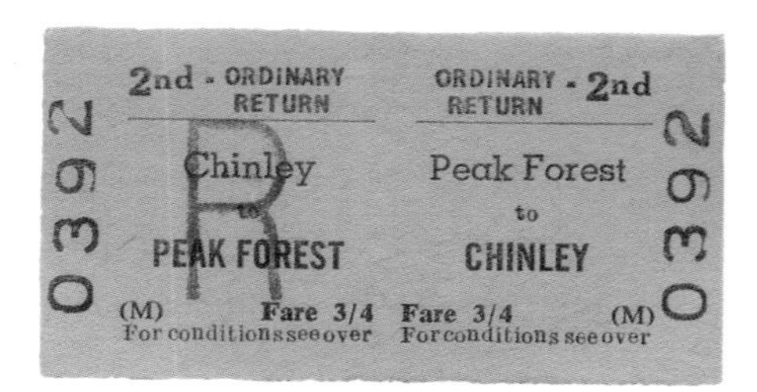

The first Brush Type 2 A1A-A1A locomotive entered service in October 1957 at Stratford depot, east London, and during the class's early years the vast bulk was based on the Eastern Region, mostly in East Anglia, or at Darnall shed, Sheffield. They could be seen powering relatively important express workings from Liverpool Street to King's Lynn and suchlike until displaced by more powerful types, or electrification. Mirrlees, Bickerton and Day 12-cylinder engines were fitted but these were later replaced by English Electric 12SVT engines which powered four Brush traction motors. The earlier locomotives, Nos.D5500 to D5519, were nominally rated at 1,250hp while the later machines mostly produced 1,365hp, but it should be noted that there were variations. The locomotives weighed around 104 tons (again with variations) and had a maximum tractive effort of 42,000lb. Later in their careers the class spread its wings considerably, very often hauling secondary passenger services, and had regular work on the WR for a time, but was never particularly common on the LMR. The class's most prestigious duty was powering the Royal train from Liverpool Street, and from Victoria to Tattenham Corner on Derby day. However, on 11th January 1961 No.D5667 broke down while working the down 'Fenman' on which HM the Queen was travelling and the hostile press, which took a delight at sniping at BR at every opportunity, had a field day. So that was definitely the low point in the class's history! In this portrait a brace of unidentified Brush Type 2s (Class 31 under the TOPS classification) ease a long stone train off the Grassington branch at Skipton during the late summer of 1984. The overgrown Grassington branch platforms can be clearly seen, the branch having lost its passenger trains as long ago as 22nd September 1930. *Author*

Perhaps it would be wide of the mark to describe a train hauled by a Class 31 and formed of Mk.1 stock as 'luxurious' but at least the passengers would have had a reasonable amount of legroom compared to modern diesel units and no constant vibration from underfloor engines. Furthermore, there would have been plenty of space for prams and bicycles – in other words a much more civilised way to travel. Here, a Norwich to Birmingham train is seen pulling away from Melton Mowbray on 17th September 1982, with the station's graceful signal box prominent on the left of the shot. Motive power is provided by No.31 236 which dated from November 1960 when it entered traffic as No.D5663 at March shed. It was later modified for electric train heating, becoming No.31 433, and subsequently became part of the Civil Engineer's pool of dedicated locomotives. *John Chalcraft*

2nd-SINGLE SINGLE-2nd
5550 5550
Melton Mowbray (Town) to
Melton Mowbray (Town) Melton Mowbray (Town)
Birmingham (N. St.) Birmingham (N. St.)
BIRMINGHAM (NEW STREET)
via Leicester & Nuneaton
(M) Fare (M)
For conditions see over For conditions see over

The British Transport Commission approved various orders for DMUs at a meeting on 2nd December 1954 and it was decided that the Gloucester Railway Carriage & Wagon Co. (GRCW) would construct a batch of 20 sets (40 vehicles) and these were initially allocated to a Manchester modernisation scheme, and also to Scotland. The prices quoted were £19,843 for a motor coach and £13,725 for a trailer car and the order was placed on 21st June 1956. In the event there was a change of plan, apparently due to the late delivery of stock for a Manchester scheme, and all of the units were initially based at Longsight until deliveries of its own sets commenced; the Gloucester units were then moved to Scotland as originally intended. On 30th January 1957 a second order was placed for another 20 sets and these were allocated to Leith Central depot in Scotland. The vehicles were actually constructed concurrently between May 1957 and March 1958; each set was equipped with two AEC 150hp engines. The DMBS vehicles weighed 30 tons 5cwt and the DTCL trailer cars 25 tons; the former accommodated 52 second class passengers while the latter could seat 12 first and 54 second class passengers. North of the border the units were principally employed on the Edinburgh to Glasgow route via Shotts and suburban workings around Edinburgh. The batches were easily distinguished from each other, the first series being fitted with a single top marker light while the later batch had two marker lights beneath the driver's windows. Cutbacks to the Scottish railway network in the Edinburgh and borders area made some units redundant and they moved southwards, working in Newcastle-upon-Tyne for a short time while other sets were sent to East Anglia. Withdrawals commenced in 1972 and the type simply faded away with the last being withdrawn in 1988. None of the Gloucester cars was ever refurbished, perhaps due to the presence of asbestos, but perhaps the type's ultimate achievement was the conversion of two cars for the use of the Eastern Region General Manager. Here, a GRCW unit forming the 4.00pm Leamington Spa (Avenue) to Nuneaton train is seen at Kenilworth Junction on 22nd July 1962. *Tommy Tomalin*

Here is a photograph of Bescot station, one of the very few pictures taken in the West Midlands submitted for this book. The train shown is the 8.35am Walsall to Birmingham New Street working and this picture was taken on 4th May 1963. The unit's single top marker light will be noted indicating that it was one of the first batch of these sets to be built. The line splits just beyond the station platforms, with the route to Walsall curving very sharply to the right while the other line goes to Wolverhampton. Bescot station clearly suffered some over-enthusiastic rationalisation at some stage to which the missing section of canopy bears testament. Note the smoke blowing across the tracks on the left – there was a huge steam shed at Bescot and the smoke was presumably a continuous feature. *Tommy Tomalin*

Manchester's Oxford Road is lined with some impressive Victorian office buildings indicating the city's status as the world's first industrial city and one of the north of England's major commercial centres. One of these buildings forms the background to this photograph of a GRCW unit forming an empty working towards Piccadilly station on 8th April 1973. Withdrawals had already commenced when this picture was taken which probably prompted the photographer to press the shutter! Some years ago a chord was laid from the Bolton to Manchester Victoria line which gave access to Oxford Road and Piccadilly, and many services which formerly used Victoria station are now routed via this link making the short, double-track section between Deansgate and Piccadilly stations one of the busiest in Great Britain.
Terry Phillips

(2299 N) (Set 2) (Set 2) (2299 N)
2nd-SINGLE SINGLE-2nd
5919
Manchester (London Road, South Junction) to
Manchester (London Rd., South Junction) Manchester (Oxford Road)
Manchester (London Rd., South Junction) Manchester (Oxford Road)
MANCHESTER (OXFORD RD.)
(M) 0/2 Fare 0/2 (M)
For conditions see over For conditions see over
5919

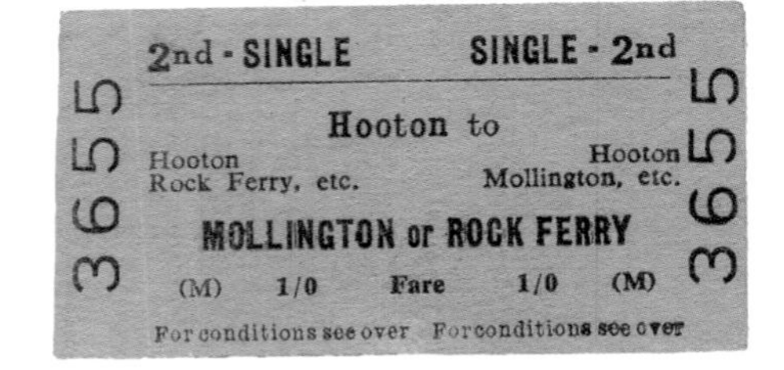

2nd - SINGLE SINGLE - 2nd
3655
Hooton to
Hooton Rock Ferry, etc.
Hooton Mollington, etc.
MOLLINGTON or ROCK FERRY
(M) 1/0 Fare 1/0 (M)
For conditions see over For conditions see over
3655

A carriage fit for the Queen. Sparkling blue paint work, including the underframe, a bright red buffer beam and, what appear to be, burnished buffers certainly made Gloucester Railway Carriage & Wagon Co. DMBS vehicle No.M50353 stand out when it was photographed at Hooton in March 1967. Unfortunately the stunning effect is neutralised to some degree by the fact that it is running with a vehicle in green livery. This coach entered traffic in September 1957 at Ryecroft (Walsall) but spent most of its career at Longsight. Withdrawn from service in July 1983 it was scrapped in June of the following year. *Dave Cobbe collection/Rail Photoprints*

Three types of DMU were built by the Birmingham Railway Carriage & Wagon Co. and these included a batch of 15 suburban sets with Derby-designed cabs for the WR (later Class 118) and 30 3-car units with 180hp Rolls Royce engines (later Class 110) built in 1961/62 for services along the Calder Valley main line and associated routes. The largest batch, however, comprised 302 vehicles (later Class 104) constructed in the late-1950s for the London Midland (LMR) and North Eastern Regions (NER) and these were fitted with 150hp Leyland engines and formed in two-, three- or four-car sets. The motor coaches weighed 31 tons while the trailer vehicles weighed 24 tons, both with some variations. All of the driving vehicles were built with a two-digit route indicator but there were variations concerning the marker lights, some cars having just a top light while others also had two lights on the cab front panelling, one above each buffer; other driving vehicles had no top light at all. There were also noticeable internal differences, cars on the LMR having wooden veneered wall panels while the NER vehicles had laminates. Later in their careers these units spread their wings and worked at many locations across Great Britain, from London to Scotland, but they will always be most identified with two routes in north-west England, the lines from Manchester Piccadilly to Buxton and from Manchester Victoria to Blackpool. Buxton depot always kept its units in particularly presentable condition and embellished them with distinctive white domes and red buffer beams. Thirteen three-car sets were dedicated to the Blackpool service and had their suspension modified; they were readily identified with a white bodyside stripe which enhanced their corporate blue livery. In this illustration a three-car unit is depicted at Countesthorpe with the 4.33pm from Rugby Midland to Leicester London Road on 22nd July 1961. Unfortunately, this was the last year of passenger services along this rural route, trains being withdrawn from 1st January 1962. Note that this particular unit is fitted with a top light and two lights (one of which is concealed by the tail lamp) on the cab front panelling. *Tommy Tomalin*

The earliest picture of an English Electric Type 4 selected for inclusion in this book is, by an amazing chance, a shot of No.D326, the locomotive that was probably one of the best-known of its class due to its involvement in the Great Train Robbery. In one of the most audacious and well-organised robberies ever carried out in Great Britain, in the early hours of 8th August 1963 a gang halted the 6.50pm Aberdeen to Glasgow and London Euston mail train at Sears Crossing, just north of Cheddington. The train had been stopped by signals which had been altered by the robbers who had placed a mask over a green light and a red indication was given by means of batteries that had been brought to the site. The locomotive crew was overpowered and forced to drive No.D326 and the first two coaches to remote Bridego bridge where they were handcuffed and told to lie down by the track while the vans were systematically stripped of banknotes, jewellery and mail estimated to be worth £2,500,000 which was a huge sum at the time. The attackers were well clear of the scene before staff on the rest of the train became suspicious and later the locomotive and two vans were moved to Cheddington for examination by detectives while another engine took the remaining vehicles on to London. Unfortunately, the mail train driver received injuries during the raid from which he never fully recovered. No.D326 is seen at Lichfield Trent Valley working a northbound train on 28th February 1961 when it was just a few months old. *Tony Sullivan*

The story of the English Electric Type 4s can be traced back to 8th December 1947, when the LMSR-designed Co-Co No.10000 emerged from Derby works, and the construction of three Southern Railway-designed 1Co-Co1 diesel-electric locomotives in the early 1950s. The LMSR built two Co-Co machines, Nos.10000/1, while Ashford constructed Nos.10201/2 with No.10203, a more powerful example, being built at Brighton. When these locomotives were launched into passenger service it soon became clear that they were clocking up phenomenal mileages compared to their steam counterparts, in some cases double the mileage attained by steam locomotives used on similar work. When BR invited tenders for 174 pilot scheme locomotives in various power classifications English Electric proposed a 2,000hp 1Co-Co1 design with a Mk.II version of the 16SVT power plant already employed on No.10203; the body styling, however, was based on the two LMSR locomotives. Ten prototypes were ordered and No.D200, which had been constructed at the company's Vulcan Foundry works, Newton-le-Willows, Lancashire, entered BR traffic at Stratford depot in March 1958. On the 18th April 1958 it worked a Liverpool Street to Norwich express, leaving London amid a fanfare of publicity. Eventually, 200 locomotives were constructed by English Electric, the vast bulk in Lancashire but a batch of 20 was built by Robert Stephenson & Hawthorns Ltd., at Darlington. The class became one of the favourite diesel classes among enthusiasts, this being reflected in the large number of pictures of these machines submitted for inclusion in this book. In this illustration one of the later built members of the class is seen near Watford village, north of Northampton, with a London-bound train on 14th January 1962. The train is about to pass over a very ornate bridge, known locally as the 'Pulpit Bridge', which carried the railway over a private track. The bridge was built in 1877, its design being specified by the local peer Anthony Henley, 3rd Baron Henley of Chardstock (1825 to 1898) who lived at nearby Watford Court. It marks the point where the line crosses the estate's North Ride and was visible from the family seat. In 2011 English Heritage bestowed Grade II listed status upon the bridge. *Tommy Tomalin*

A fascinating picture of Roade station before its closure and subsequent electrification of the West Coast Main Line. On 29th April 1962 the Northampton loop line was blocked by engineering works and the some WCML trains were making a special stop at Roade for Northampton passengers. A special bus service was provided and one of the connecting buses can be seen waiting at the top of the station approach road. Here, the driver of No.D268, working a Wolverhampton to Euston express, can be seen looking towards the photographer and no doubt wishing he could be soon on his way to London – at least his train has got the 'road'. On the right of the picture workmen can be seen carrying out excavations for the forthcoming electrification which was slowly being extended southwards. There are also a number of bystanders on the approach road, no doubt railway fans attracted by the rare occurrence of main line expresses stopping at Roade station. While the government of the day was presumably happy to sanction investment in the WCML, clearly it was considered that the traffic potential of Roade station was low and it was closed from 7th September 1964. *Tommy Tomalin*

Whoosh! The English Electric Type 4s were introduced at a time when BR was still very much in the steam age, hence they were fitted with boilers for steam heating and scoops for picking up water to replenish the boiler. Here an unidentified example, working the up 'Mid-Day Scot', makes a splash as it picks up water from Dillicar troughs, just south of Tebay, on 6th August 1962. For obvious reasons water troughs needed to be located on level stretches of line and these were hard to find on the WCML north of Carnforth, but this level stretch was ideal. When southbound trains reached the troughs they had just descended from Shap summit and would normally be travelling at a considerable speed so this was a perfect spot. The location may not have been quite so favourable for northbound trains but at least they had the advantage of some minor downhill sections after breasting Grayrigg summit, thus enabling them to gain speed. *Ron Herbert*

Between Carlisle and Shap summit the line climbs virtually all of the way apart from a couple of brief level sections and the final twelve miles beyond Penrith are mostly graded at 1 in 125. Judging by the haze of fumes being emitted, No.D255 is clearly working on full power as it passes the connection to Shap quarry and approaches the summit; it was powering the up 'Royal Scot' on 20th July 1963. On weekdays at that time the 'Royal Scot' was advertised to leave Glasgow at 10.00am and, after calling at Carlisle, it was due in London Euston at 5.10pm. On Saturdays it was allowed an extra 38min, presumably to allow for congestion or engineering works, while on Sundays its schedule was massively inflated, being due off Glasgow Central at 10.00am as usual but its booked arrival time in London was at 8.20pm, with six intermediate stops. *Rodney Lissenden*

The 'Royal Scot' was probably the highest profile named train regularly hauled by English Electric Type 4s and here, in contrast to the previous shot, it is seen on the northbound run just below Shap summit on 27th July 1963. Motive power is provided by D336, a locomotive that entered service in March 1961 at Crewe and remained in service until May 1982. Note that this locomotive is displaying a much more colourful headboard than that seen in the previous picture. *Ron Herbert*

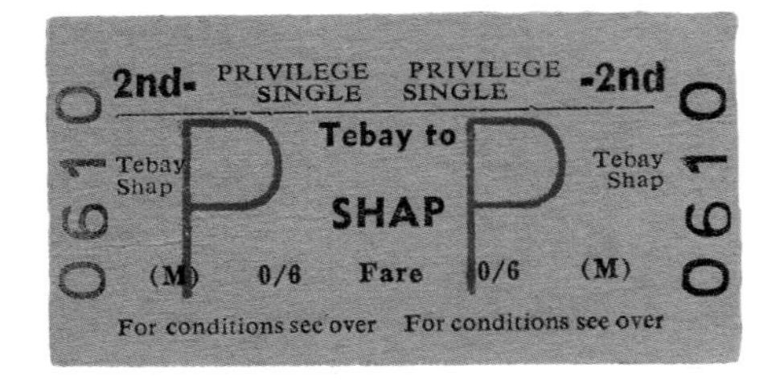

Morecambe is typical of many, once fashionable, seaside towns that have suffered drastic rationalisation of their rail services following the loss of much seasonal holiday traffic. In former days Morecambe Promenade was a sizeable station with long platforms to cater for holiday trains carrying day trippers while, despite closure to ordinary traffic in September 1958, nearby Euston Road station was available at especially busy times to relieve the pressure. In addition, frequent local electric trains connected Morecambe with Heysham and Lancaster but they were ageing, non-standard and succumbed in early 1966. In this picture No. D229 *Saxonia* is seen leaving Morecambe on 14th October 1963 and has taken the route to Lancaster Castle via Bare Lane which was not electrified. The four tracks on the extreme left are actually two separate, electrified double track routes and those furthest from the camera go to Heysham Harbour while the two tracks nearer the camera linked Morecambe with Lancaster Green Ayre station. Part of one of Euston Road's platforms is just visible on the right. The last-mentioned station closed completely from 7th September 1962, no doubt as a result of steadily declining holiday traffic. *Ron Herbert*

Northampton is a sizeable town serving a large hinterland but, at the time of writing, is not considered of sufficient importance to merit stops by WCML express services and is served solely by semi-fast EMUs. In times gone by Northampton was a stopping point for at least a small number of long distance trains, especially on Saturdays, and it was possible to catch a through service to Blackpool, Windermere or Workington and intermediate points. In this picture the 8.40am SO Carlisle to Euston, with No.D324 in charge, is depicted drawing to a halt in Northampton Castle station on 26th March 1964. This was basically a semi-fast service stopping at such places as Tebay and Hartford, its advertised arrival time in Euston being 4.45pm. There was still plenty of steam activity in the Northampton area at that time and the locomotive working a goods train in the background is Stanier Class 8F 2-8-0 No.48626. No.D324 was the last of a batch of twenty of these locomotives constructed by Robert Stephenson & Hawthorns at Darlington and this particular machine entered traffic in June 1961 and continued in service until January 1984. *Tommy Tomalin*

A member of the crew of a 350hp diesel shunter waiting in the loop stretches his legs at Grayrigg as the 11.00am Glasgow Central to Manchester Victoria train, hauled by No.D335, passes on 24th May 1964. The remains of Grayrigg station, which closed from 1st February 1954, can be discerned while the signal box is just visible in the distance; note the splendid lower quadrant signals that were still *in situ* at Grayrigg at the time of this photograph. No.D335 later became one of the last remaining Class 40s in active service, being withdrawn from capital stock in January 1985, when the last survivors, apart from No.D200 (40 122), were taken out of traffic. No.D335 (40 135) was later re-instated, and re-numbered 97 406 in the departmental series for duties in connection with the remodelling of Crewe station; it was subsequently purchased for private preservation and can be seen at the time of writing on the East Lancashire Railway. *Ron Herbert*

The Robert Stephenson connection. When the North Wales coast line was being planned it was clear that there would be two principal natural obstacles if London and Holyhead were to be connected, these being the crossing of the Conway estuary and the Menai Strait. Robert Stephenson proposed the novel idea of tubular beams within which trains would run, and in order to evaluate the practicality of this revolutionary idea it was decided to tackle the crossing of the Conway estuary first of all, this being a much easier task from the civil engineering point of view. The first of the wrought iron tubes was in position by April 1848 and the inaugural trains were able to pass through soon afterwards. The bridge has crenellated piers skilfully designed to blend with Conway castle, the outer defences of which were pierced to provide room for the tracks. Here, an unidentified eastbound express, headed by No.D310, bursts out of the up tube and into daylight on 30th May 1966. Co-incidentally, the locomotive was one of those constructed by Robert Stephenson & Hawthorns Ltd. at Darlington. *Tommy Tomalin*

0195 **2nd-SINGLE SINGLE-2nd** 0195

Menai Bridge to

Menai Bridge Conway — Menai Bridge Conway

CONWAY

(M) 4/0 Fare 4/0 (M)

For conditions see over For conditions see over

When this picture of No.D331 powering a ballast train was taken between Chinley North Junction and Chinley station on 20th March 1968, restaurant car expresses between London St. Pancras and Manchester Central via Matlock were still using this former Midland Railway route. This long-established service was in its death throes, however, because the line between Chinley and Matlock was closed from 1st July 1968 and Manchester Central station despatched its last train in early May 1969. The signals in the background indicate the 'main' line to Matlock while the secondary route to Sheffield diverged to the left, but today the Sheffield line is the principal route while the former tracks to Matlock now only provide access to quarries in the Peak Forest and Buxton areas. A reversal of fortunes one might say. The photographer recorded that this train emanated from the Matlock line and crossed over to the slow lines at Chinley North Junction; the signal box is just visible in the middle of the picture. What a pity the sun did not deign to shine on the train! *Tommy Tomalin*

Flaming June at Appleby. Photographed on a damp 2nd June 1976, a heavy goods train heads southwards behind No.40 172 which has a 'dead' Class 25 No.25 072 in its consist. The Class 25 was fortunate enough to survive into preservation but the Class 40 was not so lucky, being broken-up at Doncaster works in February 1984. The signal box in view is Appleby North which replaced an earlier structure destroyed by fire in June 1951. The replacement box was brought into commission in 1951 and positioned in the fork of the junction unlike its predecessor which had been on the west side of the line north of the down platform. This new box controlled the connection into the yard and spur to the former Penrith to Kirkby Stephen line; the spur never carried timetabled passenger trains. *Tommy Tomalin*

The Manchester to Leeds route via Huddersfield was one of the last stamping grounds of the Class 40s where they undertook all manner of duties ranging from menial goods trains to express passenger workings when the rostered motive became 'unavailable' at the last minute. Certainly, during the late 1970s and early 1980s the majority of Saturday holiday 'extras' would be likely to produce a Class 40, especially if the motive power department was suffering from one of its periodical shortages of locomotives. Here, the early evening sunshine beautifully illuminates No.40 092 as it passes through the remains of Diggle station on 19th August 1978 with the 1.44pm SO Llandudno to York. The photographer comments that he spent the night camped in a nearby field, his sleep being interrupted in the early hours by a succession of 40s growling up the bank from Manchester with newspaper and parcels trains. *Chris Evans*

The 11.11am Manchester Victoria to Holyhead train, with No.40 013 at its head, awaits departure from Victoria station on 21st August 1978. The train is standing at Platform 11 Middle which was 2,194 feet-long and Great Britain's longest railway platform connecting Victoria and Exchange stations. Upon departure the train would have passed through Exchange station on the middle road and, similarly, trains leaving Exchange and heading eastwards passed through Victoria on a middle road. The rolling stock depicted here has since become a thing of the past and the BRUTE trolleys have gone the same way. Manchester Victoria station was always a bustling hive of activity after 10.00pm when the newspapers started to arrive for transhipment on to waiting overnight trains. *Chris Evans*

The Settle and Carlisle is another line with which the English Electric Type 4s (Class 40s) were particularly associated, especially in their final years, and many of the following photographs in this section illustrate these machines on that classic route. In this picture an unidentified member of the class has just topped Ais Gill summit, out of sight beyond the far roadbridge, with a northbound goods train and begins the very long decent towards Appleby in July 1979; much of the train's consist appears to be wagons of china clay covered with tarpaulins. The bare moorland on the left is Abbotside Common which rises to a height of 2,186 feet above sea level while the highest point on Widdale Fell, in the far distance, is 2,203 feet high. This picture was taken from the slopes of Wild Boar Fell. *Author*

Another photograph taken from Wild Boar Fell, this time looking northwards towards Kirkby Stephen, and here another Class 40 is shown coming up the 1 in 100 gradient along Mallerstang Common and passing over the viaduct that carries the railway across Ais Gill beck. The beck feeds into the river Eden, the course of which is indicated by the rows of trees towards the right of the shot. There are also one or two trees alongside the Moorcock to Kirkby Stephen road which runs along the bottom of the valley in contrast to the railway high up on a ledge on the hillside, and affording railway passengers the bonus of magnificent views unobtainable from the road. This photograph was also taken in July 1979. *Author*

The Manchester to Leeds line via Huddersfield is undoubtedly one of the most photogenic featured in this album with splendid scenery across the Pennines and steep gradients in both directions. The author well remembers the route in steam days when Farnley Junction 'Jubilees', such as *Minotaur, Napier* and *Resolution* were regular performers on Liverpool to Hull trains, so it has a special place in his affections. Steam working on fast passenger trains was virtually eliminated overnight when the 'Trans-Pennine' DMUs were introduced from 2nd January 1961, with the Liverpool to Newcastle-upon-Tyne trains being turned over to the English Electric Type 4s from the same date. The latter could still be seen on the Newcastle trains well into the 1980s, deputising for the more powerful BR/Sulzer Type 4s (later classes 45/46) when the motive power situation reached a low ebb. In addition to occasional sorties on the principal passenger trains and, of course, on everyday goods duties, the English Electric Type 4s (later Class 40) were the mainstay of summer Saturday extras taking excited holiday-makers to traditional resorts such as Llandudno and Scarborough. In this photograph, which dates from August 1982, an unidentified Class 40 rumbles across the magnificent Saddleworth viaduct with a train bound for Manchester – could one wish for a more appealing vista? *Author*

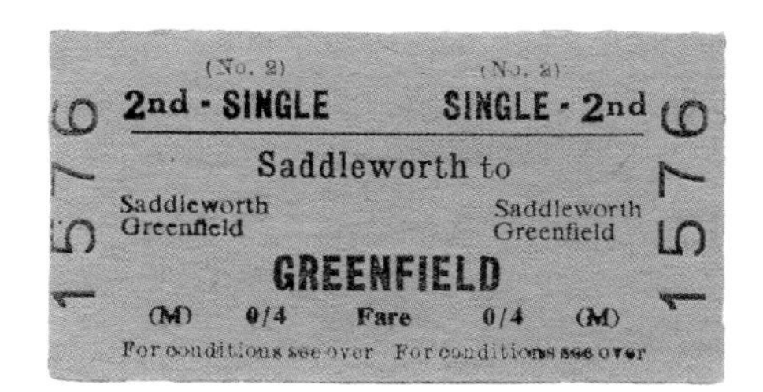

The 1983 Easter week end was one of almost unprecedented activity on the S&C line, a result of the WCML being completely closed between Preston and Penrith due to bridge replacement works and all services were diverted via Blackburn and Settle following reversal at Preston, and vice versa. In order to ensure that the operation went smoothly Garsdale signal box was opened especially and stand-by locomotives were on hand at Blea Moor to deal with any emergencies. A large number of class 47s was available at Carlisle to work southwards but by late on the morning of Saturday 2nd April Carlisle was running short of suitable motive power and undoubtedly the highlight of the day was the appearance of No.40 152 which was pressed into service on the up 'Royal Scot' despite the fact that the train was formed of air conditioned stock which the Class 40 would have been unable to heat. The Class 40 apparently remained on the diagram and returned to Carlisle with the 12.45pm *ex*-Euston, no doubt pleasing many enthusiasts but the thoughts of the ordinary, fare paying passengers, condemned to spend three hours on a cold train, are not known. Here, No.40 152 rounds the curve through Dent on its return run. Other 40s seen on the same day included No.40 074 on the 8.14am Perth to Manchester Red Bank sidings empty van train and Nos.40 082 and 40 129, both of which were employed on stand-by duties at Blea Moor. *Rodney Lissenden*

Photographed in superb autumn low lighting conditions, Class 40 No.40 063 was captured at Manchester Victoria in September 1983 in charge of a van train. The train has just passed through the ruins of the old Exchange station, whose footbridge is just visible behind West Junction signal box, and will take the middle road through Victoria. The Mk. II Inter City coaches on the extreme left are standing at Platform 11 Middle and were, perhaps, forming a train to Glasgow or another distant destination. The tightly curved tracks in front of the signal box formed the middle roads through Victoria station onto which No.40 063 would have converged. *Author*

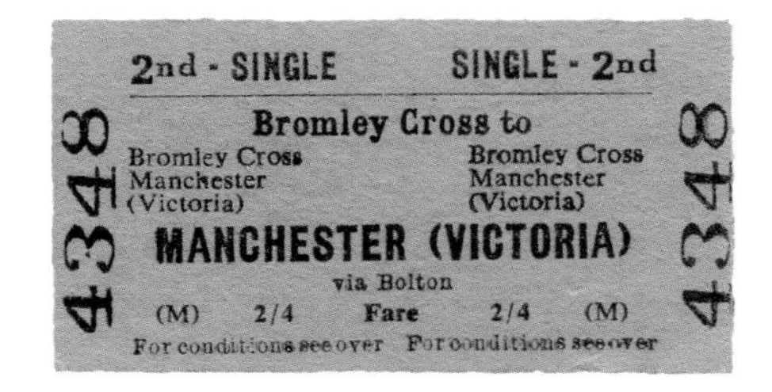

A glorious spring day at Lunds – 22nd April 1984. After 15 miles of unrelenting adverse gradients all of the way from Appleby, the 8.14am Perth to Manchester van train with No.40 060 in command takes advantage of a brief dip after breasting Ais Gill summit and approaches the 106 yards-long Shotlock Hill tunnel. No.40 060 is of particular interest because it was one of an early batch of seven of these machines allocated to Haymarket shed, Edinburgh, when new and subsequently fitted with non-standard headcode panels by the Scottish Region. Later in its career it entered departmental service as No. 97 405 for further service in connection with the rebuilding of Crewe station. *Author*

The hard work is over for No.40 015, formerly *Aquitania,* as it crosses Smardale viaduct with a lengthy King's Cross to Carlisle special train on 24th April 1984. The viaduct, which is 237 yards-long and consists of twelve 45ft-wide arches, carries the line across Scandal beck and is the tallest on the S&C line. The line of trees on the left of the picture marks the course of the old Kirkby Stephen to Tebay route which lost its regular passenger trains in 1952 but continued in use for goods workings and, at the height of the summer season, holiday trains from the north-east to Blackpool until early 1962. This line passed beneath the southernmost arch of the viaduct. The locomotive appears to be carrying 'homemade' nameplates. *Tommy Tomalin*

Many hundreds of photographs of Class 40s must have been taken at the former Appleby West station over the years but here, for a change, is a shot of a Class 40 passing through the former Appleby East on the remaining stub of the branch to Warcop. This picture shows No.40 034, formerly *Accra,* hauling the 7.30am Warcop to Stranraer Harbour, one of the extremely infrequent army specials which was presumably conveying troops for service in Northern Ireland; this portrait was taken on 9th June 1984. The photographer comments that the secondman on the engine had to open the gates across a local lane. This line was formerly part of the spectacular Penrith to Barnard Castle line which traversed the remote North Pennines and reached a height of 1,370 feet above sea level. It was closed as a through route in early 1962 but the section from Appleby to Merrygill quarry, south of Kirkby Stephen, lasted until 31st October 1974 from which date only the spur to Warcop remained for military purposes. This final stretch is thought to have closed completely to ordinary traffic in the 1990s but a section has since been taken over by a preservation society. *Chris Evans*

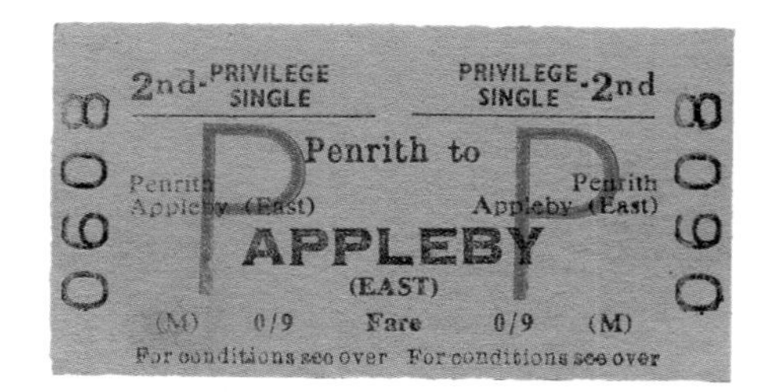

In the 1960s BR's management in Manchester was focused on the electrification of the WCML and, especially, presenting the newly reconstructed Piccadilly station as a showpiece for the modern railway. The fact that no part of the new station was actually in Piccadilly didn't seem to worry them! Two of Manchester's other terminal stations were closed leaving Victoria to the north of the city centre to become an almost forgotten Cinderella. Virtually no money appears to have been spent on Victoria for many years, apart from the installation of colour light signalling, cleaning the facade and new booths for the ticket collectors, none of which really brightened up the dilapidated passenger facilities for the travelling public. Here, in this picture taken in September 1984, No.40 082, hauling a train of tank wagons, gathers speed on the eastbound through line before assaulting the stiff 1 in 59 climb to Miles Platting which begins at the platform end. *Author*

3rd-SINGLE SINGLE-3rd
Walkden (High Level) to
Walkden (H.L.) Manchester (Vic.) Walkden (H.L.) Manchester (Vic.)
MANCHESTER (Victoria)
(M) 1/4 FARE 1/4 (M)
For conditions see over For conditions see over
2646 2646

A few minutes before this picture was taken the Ais Gill area had suffered a deluge that was quite something even by the exceptional standards of the S&C line! Luckily, the downpour stopped just before the 10.40am Carlisle to Leeds train hove into view with No.D200 (alias No.40 122) at its head and, astonishingly, the sun seems to be shining on Wild Boar Fell in the background; this portrait was taken in May 1985. No.40 122, the historic doyen of the class, was withdrawn from traffic in August 1981 and unceremoniously dumped at Carlisle awaiting disposal. There was an outcry from railway enthusiasts up and down the country when it became clear there was a distinct possibility that the machine could be scrapped and they launched a campaign to save it from destruction. Wiser counsels prevailed and No.40 122 was reinstated to traffic on 24th April 1983, moved to Toton for repairs, which included a power unit exchange with No.40 076, and the overhaul of bogies and numerous electrical components. It was certainly a day to remember when, on 22nd July 1983, No.40 122 emerged in green livery sporting both its old and TOPS numbers, the latter number being available due to the early withdrawal of D322 following accident damage. D200 was eventually withdrawn in May 1988, long after other members of the class had been retired, and its future is assured as part of the National Collection. *Author*

When the surviving Class 40s, apart from No.D200 (40 122), were taken out of traffic in early 1985 four were retained for departmental work in connection with the remodelling of Crewe station and other miscellaneous duties. The locomotives involved were Nos.40 012, 40 060, 40 118 and 40 135 which were renumbered respectively 97 407, 97 405, 97 408 and 97 406. The first mentioned locomotive is depicted in this photograph stabled at Preston Dock Street sidings on 26th August 1985 in company with an unidentified Class 47. The machine is displaying the name it originally bore, *Aureol,* and various numbers it carried during its career. One wonders how many less knowledgeable depot and yard shunters were puzzled when they were told that 'No.212' was coming on depot. *Ron Herbert*

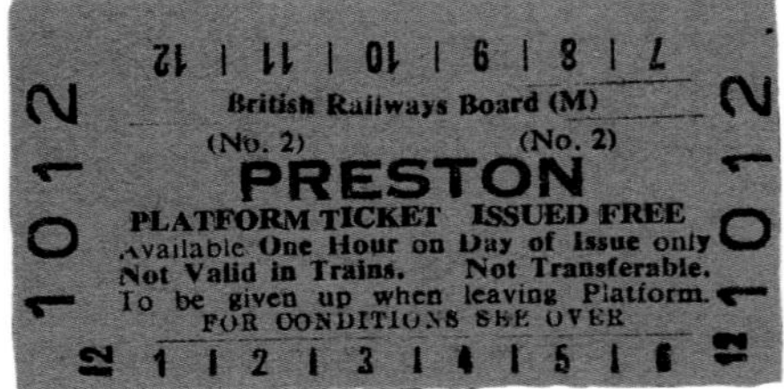

Hindsight is a wonderful thing, and there is no doubt that with the benefit of hindsight the British Transport Commission would never have allowed the proposal to build the Metro-Vick Co-Bos to progress beyond the drawing board stage. Twenty 1,200hp Type 2 locomotives, Nos.D5700 to D5719, were supplied by Metropolitan-Vickers Electrical Co. Ltd.. who manufactured the electrical equipment while mechanical parts were made by one of its subsidiaries. These locomotives, which weighed 97 tons, employed a two-stroke Crossley Vee-8 engine which was fitted for comparison purposes with conventional engines; perhaps their most remarkable feature was their novel Co-Bo wheel arrangement. The machines were built at Metro-Vick's Bowesfield works at Stockton-on-Tees and it was intended that the entire fleet would be allocated to Derby shed for passenger and freight duties on the LMR's Midland Division. The first locomotives entered service on St. Pancras to Manchester Central trains via the Peak route but the class gained a higher profile when it was booked to operate the prestigious 'Condor' overnight freight service from Hendon to Glasgow via Settle, with two locomotives working in tandem, this working being introduced on 15th March 1959. The class's performance in service was abysmal, however, and its chronic unreliability resulted in its replacement on Moorgate rush-hour trains by Fowler 2-6-2Ts and Stanier Class 5MTs on the 'Condor'. The last example was delivered from the manufacturer in October 1959 but by the following June no fewer than 17 locomotives were out of service at Cricklewood or Derby depots and some subsequently spent periods in store at Longtown, near Carlisle, while the LMR checked the guarantee(!) and tried to find solutions to their many problems. It was decided to return them to the maker's works at Dukinfield, near Manchester, and at least 10 machines had arrived there by mid-October 1961, many having spent more time out of traffic than in revenue earning service. After modification they were banished to Barrow-in-Furness shed for use on secondary passenger and goods trains in that area but never covered themselves in glory, and the entire class was withdrawn in 1967/68 when no doubt engine crews at Barrow and other depots breathed a sigh of relief. In this picture No.D5715 is seen at Green Road station, between Barrow-in-Furness and Millom, with the 9.50am Manchester Victoria to Workington Main train on 6th May 1963; note the shed code stencilled on the cab front sheeting. This machine certainly had a chequered history, entering service at Derby in April 1959 but stored from February 1961. It was noted being hauled to Dukinfield on 19th October 1961 and re-entered traffic after modification in February 1962. It spent another period out of use from July 1966 until February 1968 but was withdrawn three months later and cut-up in September 1968 at McWilliam's scrap yard at Shettleston near Glasgow. *Noel Machell*

The 9.53am Workington Main to Carnforth train, with Metro-Vick Type 2 Co-Bo No.D5706 in charge, is depicted shortly after leaving Askam, also on 6th May 1963. This train was certainly not intended for passengers in a hurry because it took no less than 3hrs. 28min. to cover the 81 miles between those two points. During the height of the summer it was extended to Manchester Victoria where its booked arrival time was 3.30pm. The train may have been 'timed' for steam traction because it included extended stops at both Millom and Barrow, presumably to take water. No.D5706 entered traffic in December 1958 and achieved less than ten years nominally in service, being withdrawn in September 1968; it was scrapped at Cashmore's, Great Bridge, yard in October 1969. *Noel Machell*

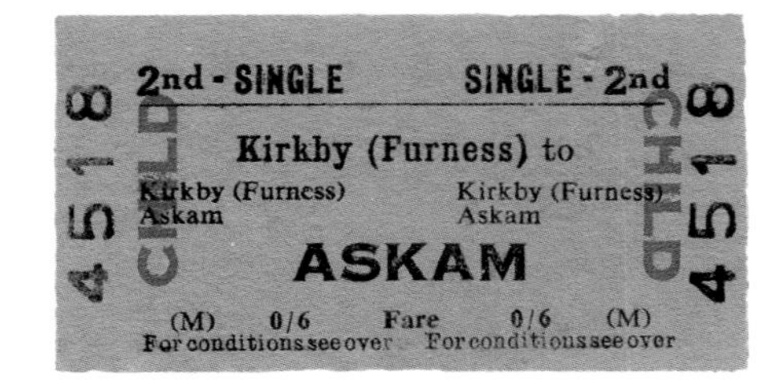

A scene near Greenodd, on the Ulverston to Lake Side branch, showing a pair of Metro-Vick Type 2s, Nos.D5718 and D5710, crossing the viaduct that carries the track over the river Leven. The train is the 7.10pm Lake Side to Barrow-in-Furness, formed of non-corridor stock, and this picture was taken on 2nd June 1963. Many services on the branch ran to and from either Morecambe or Preston and were presumably aimed at people who wanted a day out in the Lake District, but this train ran to Barrow probably because the locomotives and coaches were based at that location. When No.D5710 returned to Barrow it is likely the fitters would have had some work to do because it appears to have failed earlier in the day and No.D5718 had been summoned as a replacement; certainly its open cab door suggests there was no crew aboard. These unpredictable Type 2s regularly worked in tandem on the 'Condor' but were normally used singly following their transfer to Barrow. This interesting branch, from which daily services were withdrawn on 26th September 1938, had its summer only trains re-instated after the end of the Second World War. These later fell victim to the Beeching axe, this seasonal service being withdrawn from 6th September 1965. A road scheme along part of the track bed scuppered plans by preservationists to save the entire line but at least the section from Lake Side to Haverthwaite survives. *Noel Machell*

A good impersonation. D5700, working the 6.50pm Heysham to Corkickle oil tank train, provides an exhaust worthy of an 8F steam locomotive as it passes Hest Bank on 13th July 1964. The train is proceeding along the London Euston to Glasgow main line which for generations of railway aficionados has been known as the West Coast Main Line. This has always been something of a misnomer because the brief section near Hest Bank is the only part of the line that actually runs within sight of the sea and then only for a few hundred yards. There used to be a station at Hest Bank but it was closed from 3rd February 1969. *Noel Machell*

The British Transport Commission ordered 20 'pilot scheme' Birmingham Railway Carriage & Wagon Ltd. (BRCW) 1,160hp Type 2s, Nos.D5300 to D5319, these being equipped with a Sulzer 6LDA28 engine and four Crompton Parkinson traction motors. The first locomotive was delivered to Hornsey depot on the ER in July 1958 for evaluation, the final locomotive arriving at Hornsey from the manufacturers in March 1959. A further batch, consisting of 27 locomotives, Nos. D5320 to D5346, was delivered to the Scottish Region in 1959 and during the following year it was decided to concentrate the entire class in Scotland, and in the mid-1960s they were based at Haymarket and Inverness depots. No.D5317, seen in this picture at Carlisle on 18th June 1968, was probably based at Haymarket at this time and had just been detached from the 2.55pm Edinburgh to Carlisle via the Waverley route. Apart from the first year or so this machine spent its entire working life on the Scottish Region, ending its career at Inverness in August 1977 and was broken-up at Glasgow works in February 1978. Regrettably, the legendary Waverley route was closed to passenger traffic from 6th January 1969, just six months after this picture was taken, and appearances of BRCW Type 2s in Carlisle were probably much reduced after that date. *Terry Phillips*

BRCW Type 2 No.D5388, pictured here passing Gretton, between Kettering and Melton Mowbray, with a northbound late afternoon goods working on 6th November 1965 was one of a batch of 69 locomotives ordered in 1960. Nos. D5347 to D5369 were earmarked for the ScR, Nos. D5370 to D5378 were ordered for Thornaby shed on the North Eastern Region, while Nos. D5379 to D5415 were allocated to Leicester and Cricklewood sheds for use on the former Midland lines. Deliveries started from BRCW's Smethwick works in June 1961 and continued until the last locomotive was taken into BR stock in October 1962. This later series of BRCW Type 2s had uprated 6LDA28-B engines which produced 1,250hp and were therefore more powerful than the earlier batches; unlike the first series (D5300 to D5346) they had GEC traction motors. The machines were fitted with four digit headcode panels positioned in the roof above the driver's windows, rather than discs, and this was the principal external difference between the batches. Eventually all 69 locomotives were based in Scotland and No.D5388, which was later re-numbered 27 049, lasted in service until April 1987. The nose-end communicating doors fitted were rarely used and later sealed out of use. Passenger services were withdrawn from Gretton station and nearby Corby from 18th April 1966, but the line remained in use for freight traffic and regular services have now been restored to Corby, but Gretton has not been so fortunate. *Tommy Tomalin*

A stranger on the Settle and Carlisle. No.27 030, working a southbound ballast train on 26th April 1984, passes the Ribblesdale Lime Company's disused sidings at Helwith Bridge. Originally No.D5377 this locomotive entered service in February 1962 at Thornaby depot, was re-numbered under the TOPS scheme in September 1974 and remained in traffic until withdrawn from Glasgow (Eastfield) shed in April 1986. These locomotives sometimes worked up the S&C line from Carlisle to Appleby on goods workings but the appearance of one these machines at the southern end of the line was quite remarkable and a real bonus for the photographer. *Tommy Tomalin*

A total of 151 BR/Sulzer Type 2 Bo-Bo locomotives (later Class 24) was built at Crewe, Derby and Darlington works; the number series was D5000 to D5150. They were the first main line diesel locomotives to be constructed at Darlington for use on BR. The locomotives were powered by a 1,160hp Sulzer 6LDA28 engine and had four British Thomson Houston traction motors. The initial batch of 114 was constructed with train classification discs while Nos.D5114 to D5150 had roof mounted headcode boxes giving them a much different appearance, very similar to the Class 25s. The first 20 locomotives had been destined for use on the LMR but around 15 were temporarily moved to the Southern Region (SR) when that region found itself short of diesel motive power due to the late delivery of its fleet of BRCW Type 3s. They proved to be a mixed blessing on the SR due to their axle loading and had to have their train heating boilers temporarily removed before they could be used. The widespread allocation of the class meant that they could be observed in many parts of the country, especially in the London area, where Finsbury Park and Willesden had large allocations, and Scotland, while a considerable number was based at Gateshead. Nos.D5096 to D5113 were allocated to the last mentioned shed and modified with an additional compressor for working the Tyne Dock to Consett iron ore trains which were formed of specially dedicated hopper wagons. The very last Class 24 in traffic was No.24 081, based at Crewe diesel depot, and this outlasted other members of the class by a considerable period, thus gaining celebrity status. In this shot, taken at Derby works on 25th May 1959, No.D5018 has just emerged into daylight for the first time and is seen outside the test house in red oxide primer paint before being put through its paces. Later allocated to Crewe diesel depot it was destined to last in traffic for a relatively short time, being withdrawn from Eastfield shed, Glasgow, in August 1975. A fitter can be seen standing in the cab nearest to the camera putting the finishing touches to the door frame. *R.C. Riley*

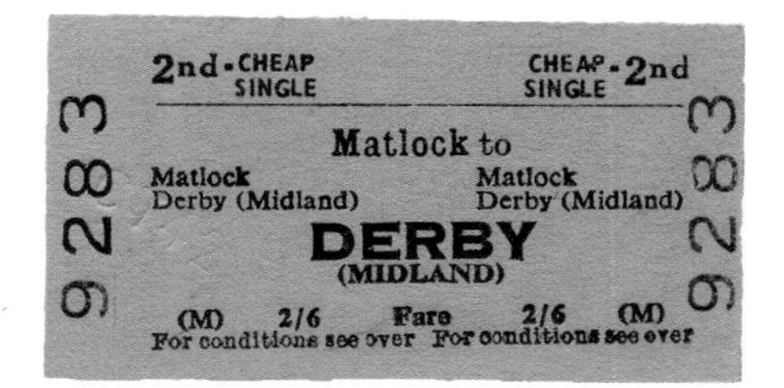

The finished product. A boy's attention is captured by a driver sitting in the rear cab of BR/Sulzer Type 2 No.D5022 which was photographed at Derby on 27th September 1959. Another locomotive is just creeping into the shot on the right of the picture and this is one of those Metrovick Co-Bos which were one of BR's most disastrous investments. No.D5022 looks presentable enough with its smart green livery and grey roof, and the grey body stripes certainly enhance its appearance but were no doubt prone to be covered with grime very quickly once the locomotive entered everyday service. No.D5022 started its life at Norwich and was eventually withdrawn from traffic at Longsight, Manchester, in January 1976.
R.C. Riley

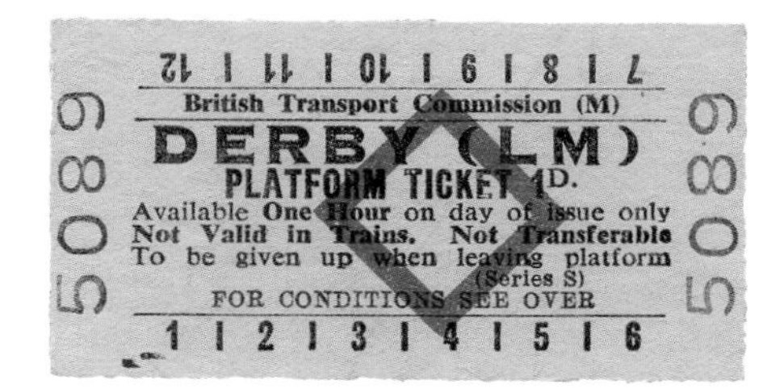

An outer suburban train, probably from Northampton, is seen passing Camden motive power depot behind No.D5146 on 3rd June 1962; note that the formation includes both corridor and non-corridor coaches of LMSR design. No.D5146 entered traffic in December 1960 and by that time the locomotives' headcode discs had been superseded by roof mounted headcode boxes which dramatically altered their appearance to closely resemble Class 25s, as previously stated. This picture appears to have been taken from the roof of Camden shed and shows Primrose Hill station, which was served by trains on the North London Line, and the distinctive girder bridge that carries Regents Park Road across the railway. It is said that many residents in this affluent area of north London objected to the smoke being emitted from steam locomotives stabled at Camden shed and their protests may have hastened the closure of this celebrated depot. *R.C. Riley*

A further view of a BR/Sulzer Type 2 in action in the Euston area and this August 1965 picture shows No.D5019 apparently engaged on shunting empty stock at the nearby carriage shed which is just out of view beyond the bridge. The photographer seems to have picked his spot perfectly at a location that presents huge challenges to railway photographers due to the many structures supporting the overhead line equipment. The dirty appearance of the locomotive is emphasised by the grey bodyside bands which undoubtedly look fine when a locomotive has just been released from the paint shop (see a previous illustration) but really needed to be kept clean! *David Cobbe collection/Rail Photoprints*

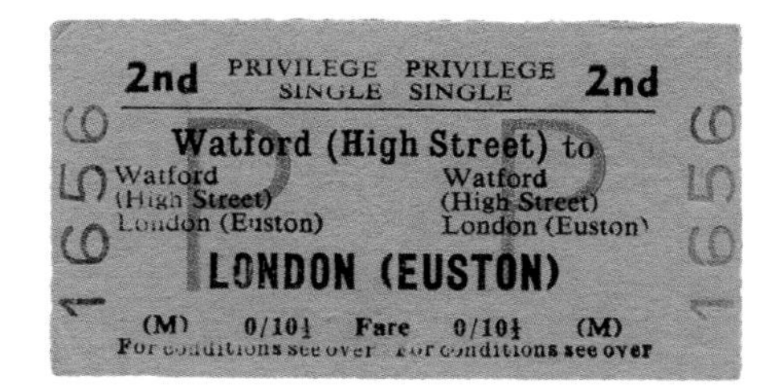

A total of 327 of the later series of BR/Sulzer Type 2s (which became Class 25) was constructed in BR workshops at Crewe, Darlington and Derby, and by an outside contractor, Beyer Peacock. These locomotives were fitted with the 1,250hp 6LDA28-B engine, this being an uprated version of the engine fitted to the earlier series of similar machines which later were known as Class 24s. A batch of 54 locomotives was scheduled to be built by Beyer Peacock but this firm was unable to complete the contract due to financial difficulties and 18 locomotives (Nos.D7660 to D7677) were actually built at Derby works in 1966/67. Most of these machines were fitted with 253AY motors made by Associated Electrical Industries (AEI) but the earlier locomotives, Nos.D5151 to D5175, had BTH motors. The former motor was lighter than the BTH model and this prompted the change. These locomotives could be seen at work on all BR regions, including the SR, which did not have its own allocation of this class. The earlier locomotives were fitted with gangway doors but these were very rarely used and later batches were not fitted. In this photograph two BR/Sulzer Type 2s, No.D7584 is nearest to the camera, are surrounded by all of the soot encrusted paraphernalia of the steam age as they huddle around a turntable at Derby engine shed in April 1967. Steam traction had become largely a thing of the past at Derby when this picture was taken but this vividly illustrates one of the problems associated with the changeover from steam, this being the lack of purpose-built maintenance and servicing facilities for the new traction. No.D7584 was one of the relatively few locomotives of this class built at Darlington works from where it emerged in February 1964. No.D7584 lasted in traffic as No.25 234 until March 1985 but it survived intact until cut-up by Vic Berry & Co. of Leicester in May 1989. *Mike Jefferies/Rail Photoprints*

A magnificent panorama taken on the Cumbrian coast line. No.25 119, hauling an empty coal train, is seen skirting the coastline south of Harrington on 6th May 1977. A photographic masterpiece if ever there was one – need any more be said? *Tommy Tomalin*

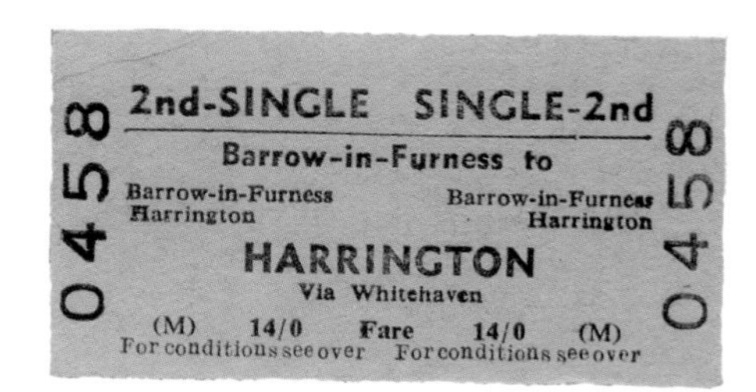

Wing sidings, about a mile south of Manton on the Melton Mowbray to Kettering line, may not have been a spectacular location but here the photographer has used his imagination to produce a really interesting and quite ingenious photograph. This shot was taken from inside the signal box and shows No.D7537 approaching the box on a routine 'day in, day out' job, working a northbound empty coal train on 29th May 1968. This locomotive has clearly been constructed without gangway doors and has its air intakes on the roof rather than on the bodyside, thus giving a much less cluttered appearance. The position of the intakes was altered on some later locomotives because tests proved that those on the sides tended to attract much dirtier air which damaged the engine and associated engine room equipment, so the design change was not simply for cosmetic reasons. *Tommy Tomalin*

The 12.06pm Heysham to Neville Hill (Leeds) oil tank train is east of the former Borwick station, between Carnforth and Wennington, on 8th June 1968 with No.D5168 piloting BR Standard Class 9F 2-10-0 No.92167, one of only two left in service on BR by that time. The pairing of a Type 2 and Class 9F on this working seems to have been fairly regular at this time but was destined not to last much longer because four days after this portrait was taken No.92167 dropped its rods while working back from Leeds, and as its boiler was also defective, it was withdrawn from traffic. The other surviving 9F, No.92160, was also withdrawn a few days later so this photograph is probably one of the last taken of a diesel and steam combination in ordinary BR service. The train was booked to be piloted between Heysham Moss and Skipton where the Type 2 diesel locomotive was detached. Normally trains conveying oil tanks require barrier wagons as a safety precaution but this working carried heavy oil and was an exception to this rule. The Type 2 was in traffic from December 1961 until November 1976 so achieved almost 15 years of active life, whereas the 9F ran for just over ten years so neither of these locomotives was a sound investment for the long suffering British taxpayer. The station at Borwick was closed as long ago as 12th September 1960. *Tommy Tomalin*

Railway photographers always had their favourite locations but Swadlincote, south-east of Burton-on-Trent, is not one that immediately springs to mind and this is the very first picture the author has seen taken at that location. This is hardly surprising because Swadlincote was served by regular passenger trains that ran on a loop line between Swadlincote Junction and Moira (Woodville Junction) and those services ran for the last time in October 1947, so determined photographers without their own transport would have to resort to local buses. Passenger trains on the nearby Burton-upon-Trent to Leicester London Road line lasted much longer and ceased to operate from 7th September 1964. Despite the withdrawal of regular timetabled services on the Swadlincote loop line BR continued to run seasonal holiday trains to Blackpool until 8th September 1962. In this illustration No.D7587 is seen arriving at the local colliery with empty wagons and will doubtless depart later with another load of coal destined, perhaps, for a nearby power station. This picture was taken on 15th October 1969 and shows the Type 2 still in green livery but with all-over yellow panels which had become mandatory by that time for safety reasons. *Tommy Tomalin*

Patch painting – a dying art? The later series of BR/Sulzer Type 2 locomotives undoubtedly benefited from the re-positioning of the air intakes on the roof, a substantial aesthetic improvement, and the application of two-tone green livery which gave them a much more pleasing appearance. However, in the case of No.D7536, depicted here at Euston station on 3rd September 1970, these desirable enhancements have been totally spoilt by a large area of the bodyside that has been patch painted in completely the wrong shade of green – surely the BR painting manual instructed staff to at least use the correct specification. Well, at least this locomotive's 'three-tone' green livery looked distinctive. *Terry Phillips*

A pair of BR/Sulzer Type 2s pass Wellingborough station with a down train of Redland aggregate empty wagons on 13th May 1980; by this date these machines were known as Class 25s and the locomotives seen here are Nos.25 320 and 25 249. The wide open spaces visible in this picture indicate that Wellingborough station is on the fringe of the town and very much remote from the centre. *Chris Evans*

Photographed in almost perfect weather conditions, No.25 186 climbs the final mile or so to the summit of the 'Long Drag' on the S&C line; it is seen approaching Blea Moor on 26th March 1982. This locomotive was formerly No.D7536 which is depicted in a previous illustration taken at Euston in 1970. Constructed at Derby works in March 1965, No.25 186 was in the twilight of its career and withdrawn in November 1982, and subsequently broken-up at Swindon works in early 1987. Note the variety of vehicles forming its train, including 16-ton wagons conveying scrap metal and coal, plus a ferry van towards the rear. *Rail Photoprints*

A brace of unidentified Class 25s, hauling a block train of tank wagons, gingerly negotiate the sharp curves between the former Warrington Bank Quay (Low Level) and Arpley stations in September 1983. The train appears to be heading towards the Manchester area along the erstwhile route via Lymm. Passenger trains were withdrawn from this obscure route on 10th September 1962 but goods traffic continued for many years afterwards until the viaduct at Latchford across the Manchester Ship Canal was found to be in need of very costly repairs. Bearing in mind that the route's remaining traffic could be easily diverted to other lines, it was decided that the expenditure could not be justified and the route was closed completely east of Latchford from 7th July 1985. The building between the bridge and industrial complex beyond is part of Warrington Bank Quay station. *Author*

An absorbing night-time scene at Crewe. The railway after dark has always had an indefinable, different dimension, and in this photograph Class 25 No.25 279 is depicted at Crewe on 22nd October 1983. The nature of its working is unknown, but the post office trolley in the foreground and mail bags piled on the BRUTE trolley in the background, suggest No.25 279 was awaiting departure with a night mail train. Note the Class 304 electric unit just creeping into the shot on the left and, like the Class 25s, these units have long since disappeared from the scene; the Class 25 seen here was lucky enough to become one of the last survivors in traffic – it lasted until early 1987 – and was subsequently purchased for preservation. *Gordon Edgar/Rail Photoprints*

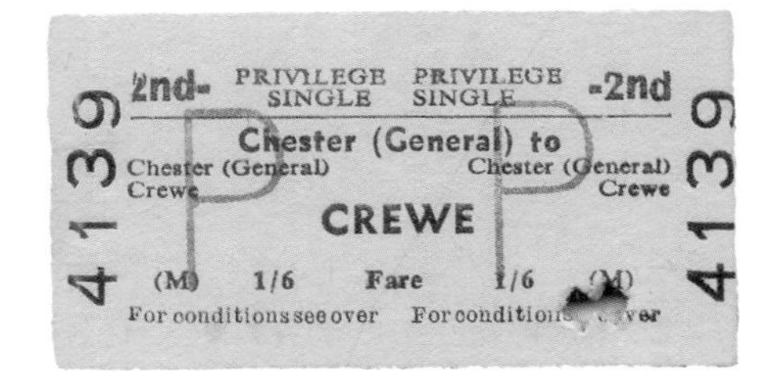

The later Derby-built 'Lightweight' DMUs were introduced in 1958 and delivered in two-, three- and four-car formations, of which the 3-car units were the smallest batch with only five being built for the ER. They were a modernised version of their predecessors, and had a revised cab and control system. A total of 333 vehicles was built during several years for the ER and LMR while the ScR and WR also had allocations at some time. In November 1959 car No.M51562 achieved its place in history when it became the 1,000th DMU vehicle to be built at Derby works and a short ceremony was held to mark the occasion. The units were mainly of aluminium construction apart from the headstocks, driving cabs and inner ends plus certain underframe components. Sets of this type were employed in many parts of Great Britain and could be observed in Devon, South Wales, Lancashire, Scotland and other areas so they were widely distributed; units working over the Central Wales line were fitted with headlights. A 2-car unit made what must have been one of the longest journeys ever undertaken by a BR DMU when it travelled to Strasbourg in 1960 for an exhibition of aluminium rolling stock. Interestingly, the DTC was merely a shell without any panelling or interior fittings so the visitors to the show could examine its method of construction; the motor coach was a complete vehicle. The author cannot recall ever travelling in Derby-built units on the continent so, presumably, if BR was hoping that orders would come flooding in from continental railways they must have been a trifle disappointed! One of these units was involved in a major tragedy when, on 19th October 1987, it ran into a collapsed bridge at Glanrhyd while forming the 5.27am Swansea to Shrewsbury train; regrettably four people lost their lives in the accident. The largely alloy construction of these units was a major factor in their long service, few being withdrawn until 1990. Thereafter, the type was rapidly taken out of traffic when an accident apparently revealed the brittle nature of the ageing alloy and the last survived until 1993. They were not contaminated with asbestos and as a result more than two dozen were taken into departmental service. The 11.27am Oxford to Bletchley train is seen at Winslow on 5th September 1964. *Terry Phillips*

A 6-car DMU rake, comprising two 2-car Derby units plus a Metropolitan-Cammell set on the rear, is seen arriving at Menai Bridge in the summer of 1965. The destination blind is displaying 'Manchester' but the train is the 11.40am Caernarvon to Bangor which was actually an unadvertised through working that continued to Manchester as the 12.17pm from Bangor. The starting signal on the right, which seems to be in an odd position adjacent to a buffer stop, referred to Holyhead-bound trains on the main line while the 'shunt ahead' bracket signal controlled entrance to the goods yard. *Terry Phillips*

Cars built from 1960 onwards had their cab design modified to accommodate a four character headcode box in the cab roof dome while the destination blind was repositioned above the middle driver's cab window. On this occasion, however, the train is not displaying a reporting number. Here, a very long rake heads westwards past Mochdre and Pabo signal box, on the North Wales coast main line, with an unidentified excursion on 29th May 1966. The small signal box at this location was only open during the peak summer season to shorten the section between Colwyn Bay and Llandudno Junction. *Tommy Tomalin*

Photographed on a rather dull and hazy day, the 12.05pm Rawtenstall to Bury Bolton Street train, seen south of Ramsbottom, drifts down the gradient towards Bury on 11th June 1968. This line was formerly part of the route from Manchester (Clifton Junction) to Accrington via Bury and Baxenden, one of the most steeply graded lines in Lancashire, while the line to Rawtenstall was merely part of a branch that used to continue beyond there to Bacup. There was already a line connecting Manchester with Accrington, albeit by a more circuitous route via Bolton, and in the Beeching era the route via Baxenden was probably seen as a so-called 'duplicate' route, which Beeching was pledged to eliminate so it was closed from 5th December 1966. *Tommy Tomalin*

In the mid-1960s DMUs started to be painted in BR corporate blue livery and here a Derby-built unit is depicted running along the shore of Morecambe Bay and approaching Grange-over-Sands station with the 4.05pm Lancaster to Barrow-in-Furness train on 31st July 1968. Initially, units were out-shopped with a small yellow warning panel, as seen here, but later an all-over yellow panel was applied. This was the final week of steam traction on BR and this scenic route was one of the last to witness steam on local goods workings. *Tommy Tomalin*

The last throes of the Great Central. The sad story of the demise of the former Great Central line from London to Sheffield/Manchester has been well documented over the years, the first blow being struck in January 1960 when the through London to Manchester expresses ran for the last time. Most local services between Aylesbury and Sheffield ceased from 4th March 1963 while the well-patronised Sunday trains were also withdrawn, thus leaving three weekday semi-fast London to Nottingham services and a variety of overnight trains that did not contribute materially to the service. It was considered that hardship would be caused if the Rugby to Nottingham local service was axed and this continued to run until withdrawn from 5th May 1969. Here, the 1.55pm SO Nottingham Arkwright Street to Rugby Central train is seen at journey's end on 7th September 1968. *Terry Phillips*

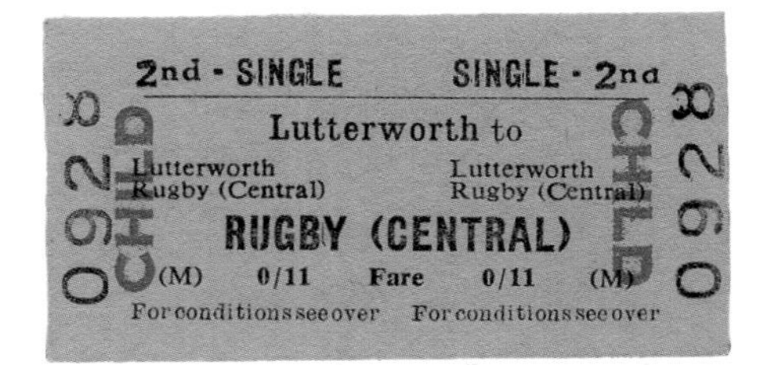

The 3.05pm Preston to Carlisle via Barrow-in-Furness train is seen departing from Whitehaven on 4th May 1977. The DMU visible in the background in the bay platform is the 4.45pm from Carlisle which terminated at Whitehaven. This station, originally named Whitehaven Bransty, was first a terminus (note the straight bay platform) opened in March 1847 when the line from Carlisle was completed but in 1852 a 1,333 yards-long single-track tunnel was opened, thus enabling trains to work through to Corkickle and points south thereof. The tunnel is largely obscured by the platform canopy in the middle of the picture. Note the droplight window bars which were a feature of stock on this route due to restricted clearances. *Tommy Tomalin*

Made in Stockport. A total of 20 Park Royal sets (later Class 103) was constructed in 1957/58 and were primarily intended to replace steam-hauled services in the Walsall area and on the Harrow & Wealdstone to Belmont branch. Whilst they have always been known as the Park Royal units they were actually built at the Crossley Motor works in Stockport, which was part of the same ACV group, and not in west London as their name implies. The units consisted of a Driving Motor Brake Second vehicle seating 52 second class passengers while the Driving Trailer Composite Lavatory coach contained 16 first and 48 second class seats; the vehicles weighed 33 tons 8 cwt. and 26 tons 7 cwt respectively. Bearing in mind they were constructed at a works better known for its production of buses perhaps it was not surprising that the units were fitted with low backed, bus type second class seats with distinctive full length chrome plated handrails. There were problems with the units' bodywork during their working lives with the result that by the end of 1972 only 12 power cars and 14 trailers were left in traffic. The final two vehicles were taken out of service in 1983 so the type did not have a particularly long life; however, some coaches saw further use as departmental vehicles. Towards the end of their careers many of the units were allocated to Chester depot and as a result they became especially associated with the North Wales coast main line. In this photograph the 4.47pm Bangor to Llandudno train is seen at Bangor on 19th July 1975 with a Park Royal unit leading a Gloucester RCW set – two of the rarer types of diesel unit working together. Bangor certainly seems to have been a happy hunting ground for DMU aficionados! *Chris Evans*

Six years after the previous shot was taken Park Royal units were still active along the North Wales coast line although by this date their numbers had declined appreciably. The 12.35pm Llandudno to Manchester Victoria is seen at Abergele & Pensarn on 8th August 1981. On this occasion the Park Royal unit is working in multiple with a Metropolitan Cammell unit; whilst the former were regarded as non-standard they were able to work in multiple with most other types. A complete unit survives in preservation at the Helston Railway in Cornwall. *Chris Evans*

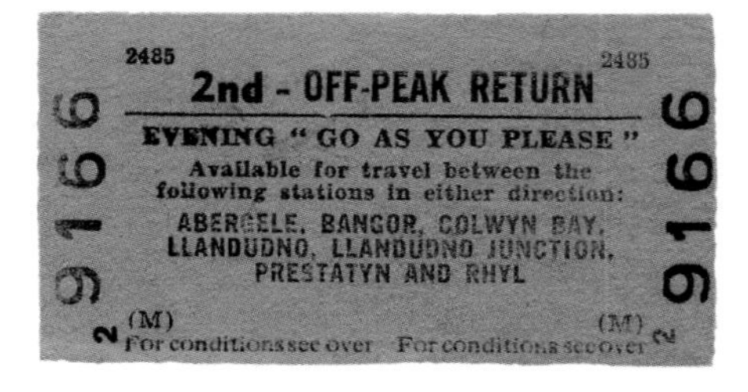

In 1958 Swindon works out-shopped the first of 49 3-car 'Cross Country' units (later Class 120) for the WR and some of their first diagrams included the Birmingham Snow Hill to South Wales trains which they took over from 9th June 1958. A further batch of seven units was constructed in 1959 specifically for the Aberdeen to Inverness run following successful trials of a unit loaned by the WR and in 1961 another series of nine units was produced, this time for use on the WR. It should be mentioned that the third batch was different in some respects to the first two series. These comfortable units, which were powered by four 150hp AEC engines, were well appointed and consisted of a Driving Motor Second Lavatory (68 seats), a Trailer Second Lavatory Buffet (60 seats plus four in the buffet section) and a Driving Motor Brake Composite (18 first class and 16 second class seats). Perhaps the most remarkable aspect of this stock was that, contrary to normal practice, the designer decided to place the first class accommodation in a motor coach rather than the trailer which would not have been subject to as much noise and vibration. In fact first class passengers travelling on this stock got a raw deal because they had to walk through the train to find the nearest lavatory while the buffet was also in an adjacent coach! The units had largely the same cab that Swindon had employed on the 'Inter City' stock built in 1956/57 for use on the Scottish Region's Edinburgh to Glasgow service but that used on the WR units had four lamps and a destination indicator and looked less austere. 'Inter City' units (later Class 126) were used on the WR for a brief period before being replaced by the 'Cross Country' units, the former being moved to Scotland to join the rest of the class. The Swindon-built units used on the WR were unique in having suspended gangways and screw link couplings and also brackets for coach letters. Another distinguishing feature was the extremely large brake vans located in the composite coach which occupied so much space there was only sufficient room for two second class seating bays with room for 16 passengers. The final batch of 1961-built units did not have a buffet, presumably because they had been found to be uneconomic, and the front ends were radically re-designed to accommodate a rather clumsy four character headcode box. In the early 1970s a substantial batch of these units was moved to Derby Etches Park depot for use on secondary services to Lincoln, Matlock and suchlike. In this illustration the 2.06pm Matlock to Derby train is seen coasting downhill from Milford tunnel towards Duffield with the Driving Motor Second Lavatory vehicle leading; this picture was taken on 11th July 1981.
Chris Evans

Parcels van No.M55997, depicted here at Newton Heath on 10th April 1971, was one of three built in 1958 by Cravens specifically for use in Cumberland where they were intended to work in multiple with early 'Derby Lightweight' units. In the event when they were delivered it was decided that they were no longer required and the vehicles spent their lives in other parts of the LMR, notably in the Manchester area. Powered by two AEC 150hp engines, these cars weighed 30 tons and were 57ft. 6ins. long. This particular vehicle, later known as a Class 129 parcels van, was withdrawn in October 1973 but not immediately scrapped. In April 1975 it was selected for conversion to a hydraulic transmission testing vehicle and renumbered RDB975385; it was eventually cut-up in May 1986. *Gordon Edgar/Rail Photoprints*

A Gloucester Railway Carriage & Wagon Co. parcels van (Class 128) stands in Manchester Victoria station on 20th August 1977. Ten of these vehicles were constructed in early 1960, six for the WR and four nominally for use in the St. Pancras outer suburban area on the LMR. They were purpose built with three sets of double doors to provide easy access. The WR cars were fitted with gangways to permit them to operate together so their external appearance was quite different to the vehicle depicted here. These vans weighed 40 tons (with variations), were 64ft. 6in. long and were powered by two Leyland Albion engines which each developed 230hp. The vehicle seen here, No.M55988, actually spent the greater part of its life in the Manchester area based at Newton Heath depot and was eventually withdrawn in October 1980; it was broken-up in March 1983. It should be noted that the engine exhaust pipes were located at the other end of the vehicle, the appearance of which would have been quite different to the view seen here. *David Cobbe collection/Rail Photoprints*

A star is born. The first of the BR/Sulzer 1Co-Co1 2,300hp locomotives, No.D1 *Scafell Pike*, looked absolutely magnificent when photographed at Derby works on 25th May 1959 following its release a few days previously for trial running; it eventually entered traffic in August 1959. These locomotives, which weighed 133 tons 3 cwt., were designed for mixed-traffic duties with a capability of hauling 660 tons at a speed of 74mph on level track. They were fitted with a Sulzer 12LDA28 twelve cylinder engine, these being supplied by the company's works at Winterthur in Switzerland, and the engine powered six Crompton Parkinson traction motors. The 'Peaks', as they were universally known, were based on experience gained from the LMSR's 1947-built Co-Co No.10000 and the Sulzer engine which had been developed prior to the Second World War and had an excellent track record on the continent. The class made its debut in passenger service on the WCML in early 1960 but was soon ousted by English Electric Type 4s and relegated to freight work from Toton depot. No.D1 lasted in traffic until October 1976 and was broken-up at the place of its birth in February 1977. *R.C. Riley*

After an initial flourish on WCML express services the early 'Peaks', which later became known as Class 44s, spent all of their remaining years on freight work, as previously mentioned, and in this picture an unidentified member of the class is seen north of Clipston & Oxendon, on the Market Harborough to Northampton line, on 12th September 1964. The locomotive is propelling a diesel brake tender, vehicles that were introduced to provide additional braking force on unfitted, or partially fitted, goods trains. Note that the tracks are on different levels and have separate bores as they pass beneath an area of high ground. The line southwards from Market Harborough climbs quite steeply and in steam days heavy goods trains had to be banked up to the summit at Kelmarsh which is located around 400 feet above sea level – note the smoke marks on the bridge.
Tommy Tomalin

Another portrait of a 'Peak' taken on the Market Harborough to Northampton line, this time north of Pitsford & Brampton; the locomotive depicted is No.D3 *Skiddaw* which was powering a very long southbound freight train on 17th October 1968. Note the train classification discs that made these early 'Peaks' so distinctive and also the corridor connection which was so rarely used. The last local passenger trains ran on this little-known line on 2nd January 1960, but some of the intermediate stations had already been closed by that time and its principal use was for freight traffic, including the distinctive coal trains with large hopper wagons that operated between collieries in the Nottinghamshire coalfield and Stonebridge Park power station. The route was used for diverted WCML services for some time afterwards, so it was quite a useful link. *Skiddaw* was in traffic from September 1959 until July 1976, this being the first of the early 'Peaks' to go for scrap; other locomotives survived on mundane Toton to Whitemoor coal trains until late 1980. *Tommy Tomalin*

Banked by GWR-designed pannier tank locomotive No.9429 (just out of the shot), 'Peak' No.D98 is seen at Bromsgrove with a northbound train on 1st October 1961. This is the earliest picture of one of the 2,500hp BR/Sulzer Type 4 locomotives submitted for publication in this album and shows the locomotive in original condition with the characteristic light grey grilles and stripe along the lower bodyside, the decorative effect of which was soon lost beneath grime, as seen here. Note the 17A (Derby) shed plate in the middle of the nose end. The principal batch of 'Peaks', Nos. D11 to D137, employed the 12LDA28-B engine which was an improved version of that fitted to the earlier locomotives; they had Crompton Parkinson traction motors. The later examples, Nos.D138 to D193, known as Class 46 in later years, were equipped with Brush traction motors. The locomotive seen here was built at Crewe, entered service in April 1961, and became No.45 059 under the TOPS computerisation policy. It was never equipped for electric train heating but at least it was bestowed with a name, becoming *Royal Engineer* in December 1966 and survived until taken out of traffic in March 1986. Perhaps it should be pointed out that at the time of this photograph Bromsgrove was just over the regional boundary on the WR but, of course, Bromsgrove came under LMR jurisdiction for many years. *Tommy Tomalin*

Photographed at East Langton, north of Market Harborough, No.D135 is depicted heading northwards on a long goods train; this picture was taken on 22nd June 1966. Later batches of these machines were fitted with centrally positioned four digit headcode panels, as seen here, in preference to the split headcode boxes. No.D135 was one of the last 'Peaks' to be built at Crewe works and entered traffic in December 1961; it was equipped with electric train heating in February 1975, was re-numbered 45 149, and lasted until September 1987. There was a wayside station at East Langton but it was closed from 1st January 1968. Note the huge hopper wagons formed immediately behind the locomotive, these apparently being of the type used to convey coal from the Nottinghamshire coalfield to Stonebridge Park power station. *Tommy Tomalin*

During 1961 Crewe works was turning out three 'Peak' locomotives a month on average, and it was only a matter of time before the class gravitated to the Settle & Carlisle line and took over the few fast passenger trains which were then being mainly worked by Gresley Class A3 Pacifics. The 'Peaks' started to appear regularly on the 'Thames–Clyde Express' from the commencement of the summer timetable on 12th June and also powered other through Leeds to Glasgow expresses sporadically from that date. From 3rd July, however, BR/Sulzer Type 4s were in complete command of all through trains on the route, including the St. Pancras to Edinburgh 'Waverley' express in both directions, but steam traction still appeared on summer Saturday and relief trains. Ironically, the 8.05am Hellifield to Carlisle local working, which had been diesel worked, reverted to steam operation at about the same time. Here, an unidentified 'Peak', hauling a mixed formation of maroon and blue/grey coaching stock, takes a northbound train across Arten Gill viaduct, between Ribblehead and Dent stations, on 9th May 1967. *Tommy Tomalin*

A colourful 'Peak'. An unidentified BR/Sulzer Type 4 is seen in primer at Derby on 13th September 1968 shortly before the application of corporate blue livery and full yellow ends. Surely, a tasteful shade of maroon would have suited these locomotives much better than blue which soon fades in everyday use. One is almost tempted to say they would have looked better running around in pink primer (with a few coats of varnish, of course!) rather than BR's rather dull and unattractive shade of all-over blue. *Terry Phillips*

When BR dispensed with steam traction in August 1968 the 'D' prefix that had hitherto been used to denote a diesel locomotive was abolished and this resulted in some of the earlier 'Peaks' being reduced to one digit only on the bodyside! No.68, seen here waiting to leave Manchester Piccadilly with the 3.17pm to Harwich Parkeston Quay on 19th June 1973, at least had two digits and also carried the name *Royal Fusilier,* and attractive regimental badges, to give it a little extra glamour. So, No.68 was quite a distinguished machine and had a reasonable innings, surviving as No.45 046 until August 1988. *Terry Phillips*

A 'Peak' at the former Peak Forest Junction. Generations of travellers between London and Manchester had a choice of routes which, needless to say, served a wide variety of intermediate stations and offered many travel opportunities. The service along the former Great Central line was withdrawn as long ago as January 1960 while trains from St. Pancras to Manchester Central via Derby lasted longer and ended when the Matlock to Chinley section was closed from 1st July 1968. A connection was retained at the northern end of the route to give access to quarries in the Peak Forest and Buxton areas (as previously mentioned), this being part of the former main line. South of Peak Forest there was a triangle that provided direct access to Buxton from both Miller's Dale station to the south on the Derby line, and Chinley to the north. This photograph shows an unidentified BR/Sulzer 'Peak' locomotive coming round the western side of the former triangle with a freight working from Buxton and passing the site of the erstwhile Peak Forest Junction. The trackbed of the old main line to Derby is on the left while the course of the former connection from Miller's Dale station to Buxton is hidden from view in a deep rock cutting above the tail end of the train. The dramatic limestone cliffs in this area give a good idea of the splendours of the old Midland Railway Peak route. This picture was taken on 22nd June 1977. *Tommy Tomalin*

The Manchester Locomotive Society
The Stevenson Locomotive Society
0018 W 561 22nd APRIL, 1961 0018
HIGH PEAK RAIL TOUR
Chinley, Edale, Peak Forest, Buxton, East Junction, Hindlow, Harpur Hill, Parsley Hay, Longcliffe, Middleton Top, Sheep Pasture Top, High Peak Junction, Cromford Wharf
SECOND CLASS For conditions see over

Generations of railway photographers have rightly complained about the violent wind and persistent heavy rain frequently experienced at Ais Gill summit on the Settle & Carlisle line but the author clearly remembers a balmy summer afternoon there in July 1979. The East Coast route was partially closed due to a rockfall in Penmanshiel tunnel and freight trains were being diverted over the Settle line, this resulting in a succession of additional workings. The train seen here is the 10.25am Nottingham to Glasgow working with an unidentified 'Peak' in charge; this train was due at Appleby at 2.15pm. Note the strange formation, the first two carriages immediately behind the locomotive being brake vehicles while those passengers in need of sustenance could apparently choose between patronising the restaurant buffet car or the miniature buffet – one wonders whether they were both manned! *Author*

Photographed on a perfect July evening the afternoon Glasgow to Nottingham passenger train with a 'Peak' in charge approaches Ais Gill summit. The first ten BR/Sulzer Type 4s (later Class 44s) were named after mountains in England and Wales and when they entered service they were commonly referred to as 'Peaks' but when the main series of these machines (later Class 45s/46s) started to be delivered the name stuck despite being somewhat inappropriate for the vast majority of those locomotives which were either unnamed or named after regiments; there was one notable exception, No. 45 022 *Lytham St. Annes*. The 'Peaks' were generally robust and reliable machines in service but, like other classes, were plagued by temperamental train heating boilers, especially in the early years. *Author*

No.45 075 awaits departure from Nottingham with the 10.25am to Glasgow Central via the Settle and Carlisle line on a freezing 9th January 1980. No prizes for guessing what type of train heating was in use on this train and there can be no doubt, judging by the amount of steam escaping from various carriages, that the Class 45's heating boiler was in good fettle. Let us hope that most of the steam reached the radiators! Released into traffic in December 1961 as No.D132, this locomotive was withdrawn from service in January 1985 but survived for almost a further two years before being broken-up at Vic Berry's, Leicester, scrap yard in October 1986. Note the vast amount of litter strewn across the tracks – surely they were not always that untidy? *Chris Evans*

Well done, Toton. No doubt thoroughly fed up with BR's drab corporate blue livery, the depot staff at Toton decided to give their Class 45 fleet a makeover, applying white stripes to the upper and lower bodysides which made them look really distinguished. Regrettably, only two locomotives, Nos.45 110 and 45 121, received the 'Toton treatment' before the depot's enterprise was brought to the attention of top management who, apparently, immediately clamped down on the initiative. What a shame! In this illustration No.45 110 is seen at Nottingham on 13th May 1980 after arrival with the 3.00pm Sheffield to St. Pancras train. *Chris Evans*

The golden age of the 'Peaks'. The 'Peaks' will always be closely identified with the Midland Main Line where they held sway for almost two decades and this photograph is a typical scene from their twilight years on that route. Photographed just north of Wellingborough, No. 45 124 is seen approaching the station with the 11.00am Sheffield to St. Pancras on 31st October 1981; the train is largely made up of Mk. 2 air-conditioned stock. The writing was on the wall for the 'Peaks' by this date, however, and 1981 proved to be their last full year in charge of the route's principal expresses, High Speed Trains being drafted in during the following year. On the right of the picture are the remains of Wellingborough locomotive shed which, in steam days, hosted such distinctive locomotive classes as the LMSR Beyer-Garratts and BR Standard Crosti-boilered Class 9F 2-10-0s, neither of which were successful designs. Other classes, however, certainly earned their keep powering heavy coal trains to keep London's fires burning. *Rodney Lissenden*

The end of the road. Photographed on 11th December 1981, which was clearly a day of arctic weather conditions, Class 45 No.45 123 *The Lancashire Fusilier* approaches Market Harborough with a southbound train of condemned coaching stock *en route* to the breaker's yard. A Crewe-built locomotive, No.45 123 entered traffic in June 1962 as No.D52 and was named in October 1963; withdrawn in September 1986 it remained intact until it was scrapped at Vic Berry's, Leicester, establishment in July 1988. The tracks on the left of the shot are those that connected the Midland main line with Northampton, a route that lost its sparse service of passenger trains as long ago as 4th January 1960. Freight traffic and occasional diverted passenger trains continued to use the route however for some years afterwards but the line was later closed completely and the tracks removed. *Chris Evans*

The 4.35pm Carlisle to Leeds train, with No.45 026 in charge, ascends the 1 in 100 gradient towards Ais Gill summit on 24th April 1984. By this date BR's avowed intention to close this legendary route had provoked an outcry and was being given considerable coverage in the media; many people, most of whom were not railway enthusiasts and had probably never heard of the line before, decided to take a trip to see if the line really was as beautiful as the hype suggested. In 1983 most trains were comprised of a paltry four or five coaches hauled by a Class 31, but by the following spring packed twelve-coach trains had become commonplace and BR was forced to lay on extra services. Many observers cast doubt on BR's estimate for the repair of the 'crumbling' Ribblehead viaduct and the line was seen as an irreplaceable part of Great Britain's national heritage which should not be destroyed. The rest, as they say, is history. *Author*

Following the class's displacement from the Midland main line in 1982 alternative work was found for many 'Peaks' on the trans-Pennine route via Huddersfield, though it has to be said that to the dismay of many enthusiasts this was at the expense of the much-loved Class 40s. The Liverpool to Newcastle-upon-Tyne service and Bangor to Scarborough workings gave employment to many 'Peaks' and Longsight and Allerton depots reportedly built up their own stocks of spares to keep the locomotives running. Here an unidentified Class 45 is depicted on the climb, mostly at 1 in 125, to Standedge tunnel; it is seen near Greenfield on a bitterly cold day in February 1986. *Author*

On 19th November 1956 a deputation of civic leaders and local MPs from along the St. Pancras to Bedford line held a meeting with Mr David Blee, General Manager of the LMR, who doubtless agreed that their service was in need of improvement but stressed that modernisation of the system was largely determined by the rate at which new rolling stock could be delivered. Perhaps as a result of the meeting dieselisation of the route moved up Mr Blee's priority list because construction of new DMUs for the line commenced in the summer of 1958 and the route's improvements included a new diesel depot at Cricklewood specifically to maintain the new units; the total cost of the line's modernisation, including the new depot, was quoted as £2.5m. Thirty 4-car units (later known as Class 127) were built at Derby works and consisted of two Driving Motor Brake Second coaches, one Trailer Second and a Trailer Second Lavatory vehicle; they were universally known as the 'Bed-Pan' stock for obvious reasons. The units, which provided 352 second class seats (later slightly reduced), were powered by 238hp Rolls Royce engines and had hydraulic transmission; they were the first DMUs to have four-digit headcode boxes. Most unusually, these units were second class only which was, perhaps, surprising bearing in mind some of the relatively prosperous middle-class commuter areas they served. The first of the brand new units reportedly entered St. Pancras on 14th May 1959 and the new stock started to appear in passenger service from 28th September 1959, albeit on existing steam timings. After several months of experience with the new DMUs it was decided to dispense with steam traction completely and introduce a full diesel service from 11th January 1960 but, alas, the DMUs had numerous teething difficulties which caused considerable dislocation to the timetable and resulted in complaints in the national press. Perhaps the complainants had overlooked the vast improvement in journey times and the frequency of trains on the route, an example being Luton which saw a staggering increase from 50 weekday trains to London to no fewer than 88. Despite the difficulties there was a general surge in passenger carryings of 19.5% in the first few weeks. The stock lasted until replaced by electric units in 1983 and a farewell tour took place on 12th March 1983, but this proved premature because the DMUs' last 'official' day in normal passenger service was 10th July. There was no further use for most of the power cars which were scrapped, but the trailers were despatched to Tyseley where some survived for a further ten years; some power cars were converted for parcels use. Here, a four-car unit forming the 3.05pm St. Pancras to Luton train is seen restarting from St. Albans on 16th July 1977. The second vehicle in the formation is a Trailer Second Lavatory carriage which originally had a mix of smoking and non-smoking accommodation in small saloons but all passengers had access to two lavatories located in the middle of the coach. *Chris Evans*

A notable success story. When this book was being written in February 2017 English Electric Type 3s (nowadays known as Class 37s) were still at work on the national system well over half a century after the first representative took to the rails in December 1960. What better recommendation could there possibly be? These 1,750hp Co-Co locomotives have an overall length of 61ft. 6in., are powered by the English Electric twelve-cylinder 12CSVT engine and have a maximum speed of 90mph; their nominal weight is 103 tons but with variations. They closely resemble the earlier English Electric 1Co-Co1 Type 4s but are shorter and lighter than those machines while their power/weight ratio is better. A total of 79 locomotives was ordered at first, mainly for mixed traffic duties on the Eastern Region, and Stratford shed, in east London, was the first to receive an allocation of the class; a total of 309 locomotives was eventually built. The class was not particularly associated with the LMR and in the mid-1960s it was largely allocated to the WR, for use on coal trains in South Wales, and the ER/NER; this may account for the paucity of pictures submitted for publication. In this picture, taken on 25th May 1963, No.D6816 is seen south of the former Charwelton station on the Great Central main line with a football special taking Manchester United supporters to Wembley. Their team pulled off an unexpected victory against Leicester City so the fans would have returned home in jubilant mood. Steam locomotives were used for the majority of football specials on that day, being especially cleaned for the occasion, but this would almost certainly have been unnecessary in the case of No.D6816 as it was almost brand new, having entered traffic in March. Interestingly, that locomotive was allocated to Darnall shed at Sheffield at the time so, presumably, the train had been routed via the Woodhead route using electric traction with engines being changed at Sheffield Victoria. Quite a fascinating route which was no doubt appreciated by the supporters! *Tommy Tomalin*

The decline of the Great Central (GC) line. Inter-regional trains were often operated on the basis of the coaching stock being supplied by the originating regions on alternate days, so this meant green-liveried SR sets provided for the Poole to Newcastle-upon-Tyne service worked to Tyneside while NER sets of maroon stock worked to the South Coast. In this portrait No.D6808 is seen at Kirkby South Junction on the former Great Central main line with the 8.30am *ex*-Newcastle on 19th June 1965; most unusually for the LMR the entire train is in uniform green livery. By the date of this photograph the Great Central route, which was regarded as an unnecessary duplicate route, was being run-down prior to closure north of Aylesbury. The local trains on this section between Sheffield and Nottingham had already been discontinued and only a few inter-regional workings and miscellaneous overnight services remained, and it is arguable whether they actually constituted a 'service'. In the winter 1964/65 LMR timetable there was a train from Sheffield to Marylebone at 12.45am but the next working southwards was not until 11.37am, this being the equivalent of the train depicted here. The 11.37am was routed via Banbury and followed the 12.30pm Nottingham-Marylebone as far as Woodford Halse, so was not an option for any passengers bound for intermediate stations to London because the next London train from Woodford Halse was at 6.51pm. The line converging from the right is the former Great Northern Leen Valley route from Langwith Junction while the converging GC line from Mansfield (note the bracket signal) is concealed by the coaches of the train. *Tommy Tomalin*

A long train of empty coal wagons, *en route* from Rose Grove to Royston, descends from Copy Pit summit towards Portsmouth on 13th June 1968. Motive power is English Electric Type 3 No.D6929 which has been disfigured by an all-over yellow warning panel. Steam traction could still be observed on this heavily graded section of line at the time of this picture and, perhaps, the photographer was hoping for a Stanier 8F. In the mid-1980s this machine was named *The Cardiff Rod Mill,* not really the most romantic name allocated to a railway locomotive but, presumably, they were among BR's regular customers. *Tommy Tomalin*

A moment in history as Class 37 No.6722 stands in Manchester Piccadilly station on 5th May 1973 after arrival with the 7.33am boat train from Harwich Parkeston Quay. This was the last time this train used the Great Northern & Great Eastern Joint Line between March and Gainsborough and also the final occasion on which GE motive power was used throughout. The photographer pointed out that the train was due in Piccadilly at 2.00pm and the station clocks suggest it must have had a very good run. From 7th May 1973 the train was re-routed via Peterborough and Nottingham to Sheffield where a reversal was necessary and a Class 45 took over. *Terry Phillips*

A journey to remember. On 1st March 1986 the author was a passenger on the morning Carlisle to Leeds train which was powered by Class 47 No.47 559. It had been a bitterly cold night in the Pennines and, after a relatively uneventful journey, the train ground to a halt at Kirkby Stephen West station which was closed to regular passenger traffic at that time. There were quite a number of railwaymen at the station and the normally deserted goods yard was a hive of activity, most of this being focused on Class 37 No.37 226 which was sandwiched between two independent snowploughs and had clearly just returned from snow clearance duties somewhere along the line; a number of BR staff were examining the snowploughs presumably to ensure they were fit to return to Carlisle. After some delay the author's train eased forward and then set back onto the down line before proceeding at a cautious pace up the bank to Ais Gill. The need for the snowploughs was revealed later when the train threaded Dentdale; drifting snow had blocked Shale cutting, near Arten Gill viaduct, and the up track was still impassable. Other vulnerable cuttings were also affected but to a lesser degree. No.47 559 gingerly proceeded to Blea Moor where, after taking the single line across Ribblehead viaduct, the signalman routed it back onto the up line and some semblance of normality resumed. Taken from the stationary train, this shot shows No.37 226 ticking over in Kirkby Stephen goods yard after clearing the line southwards, and all this effort for only four timetabled passenger workings. *Author*

A total of 35 4-car high-density, outer suburban units was constructed by Derby works in 1960 for the services radiating from Marylebone, while an additional six units were built for the Manchester to Liverpool via Warrington route but these were later transferred to Marylebone. The London area sets were built in two batches of 15 and 20 units and it appears they were delivered before the new Marylebone maintenance depot was available and were initially put to work on other lines, including St. Pancras to Bedford, before moving to Marylebone. The vehicles were 64ft. long and the motor coaches were powered by two 230hp Leyland Albion engines, so they were particularly powerful units. The Driving Motor Brake Second coaches weighed 38 tons and seated 78 second class passengers, the Trailer Second carriages weighed 29 tons and had 106 second class seats while the 30 ton Trailer Composite Lavatory vehicles seated 30 first and 40 second class passengers. The principal services operated by this stock radiated from Marylebone and ran to Aylesbury, Banbury and High Wycombe. The units, which became Class 115 under the TOPS scheme, were built without corridor connections but some were later fitted with gangways. These units had very comfortable high backed seats and were almost luxurious compared to other, much more spartan DMUs used on similar outer suburban duties in other parts of the BR network; perhaps it was just a co-incidence that the BR headquarters was just across the road from Marylebone station! The fleet was transferred to Bletchley during the 1980s and in 1987 a number of power cars were transferred to Tyseley during a major re-shuffle of the LMR's DMU fleet. These units extended their sphere of activity while based at Bletchley and worked the Barking to Gospel Oak service until displaced by class 117 units. The last Class 115 working from Marylebone occurred in July 1992 after the class had been ousted by new Class 165 units, but some lasted a little longer at Tyseley. In this illustration a Class 115 unit is depicted near Amersham forming the 10.40am Aylesbury to Marylebone train on 27th October 1983. The first three coaches are in blue and grey colours but the fourth vehicle is still in rail blue. *Tommy Tomalin*

A really powerful train. Relative to their weight the 6-car, 1,840hp 'Trans-Pennine' units introduced in 1960 were the most powerful DMUs to operate in Great Britain and, uniquely, were the only units with intermediate power cars, these being essential in view of the demanding gradients and tortuous nature of the Liverpool to Hull route across the Pennines. A total of eight units was constructed at Swindon works plus three spare vehicles but they were never kept in fixed formations. They were formed of two Driving Motor Composites and sandwiched between them were two Motor Brake Seconds, a Trailer Second and a first class buffet coach; the units provided 60 first and 232 second class seats. The earlier Swindon-built 'Inter-City' units were often criticised for their uninspiring appearance so the British Transport Commission consulted an industrial design expert who produced a much more appealing glass-fibre front end complete with wrap-around cab windows, though it has to be said that these later proved a maintenance nightmare. The coach bodies were built as a single welded structure (apart from the cab ends) and designed to withstand an end compression load of 200 tons. The first class intermediate cars were generally similar to Mk.1 loco-hauled stock, the compartments being finished with polished, veneered timber with dove grey formica being used in the corridors and vestibules. The second class accommodation was also of a high standard and both classes offered a choice of saloon and compartment seating. The buffet cars had attractive décor, offered a modest meal service, and had compartment accommodation for 18 passengers; there were also two tables next to the buffet section each with seating for four passengers. In late December 1960 a series of inaugural runs was arranged, doubtless with press publicity in mind, and the mayors of the various major cities served by the new service were invited to travel on the new trains preparatory to their full introduction on Monday 2nd January 1961. A revamped Liverpool to Newcastle-upon-Tyne service, employing English Electric Type 4s, was introduced at the same time so steam enthusiasts must have been close to despair as their favourite locomotives disappeared virtually overnight. The new units bore 'Trans-Pennine' headboards and the four intermediate vehicles also carried roof boards, so they entered service with quite a fanfare of publicity which resulted in a 45% increase in travel from Leeds and other centres on the route. The success of the new service could not last forever and in the 1970s it started to be undermined by the opening of the M62 motorway and increasing use of other, less comfortable DMU vehicles when 'Trans-Pennine' coaches were unavailable which reduced the service quality. Failures became more frequent and in 1975 the remaining buffet vehicles were withdrawn, 5-car formations becoming standard, so by this time the service had really lost its gloss. The western end of Standedge tunnel is the unmistakable location for this portrait of the 3.15pm York to Liverpool Lime Street train which is seen bursting out into daylight at Diggle on 19th August 1978. The Class 124 units had been reduced to five cars by this date; the second carriage in the formation is a MBS vehicle. *Chris Evans*

During 1977 the type was integrated with redundant WR Class 123 units and in 1979 a thorough reorganisation of all services across the Pennines resulted in the units being mainly concentrated on the Hope Valley route, operating from Manchester to Hull and Cleethorpes via Sheffield; here a Manchester-bound train is seen passing Hope station, appropriately, on 5th May 1981. Even in early May there were still patches of snow in the gullies of hills in the background. In 1981 ten of the MBS vehicles had their engines removed, thus becoming trailer brake seconds and in December 1981 the last coach to receive a heavy repair was out-shopped. In addition to trains along this line, the hybrids also had diagrams from Hull to York and in 1982 gained a regular working from Leeds to Lancaster following BR's abandonment of the Nottingham to Glasgow service via the Settle and Carlisle line; the class 123/124 hybrid units provided a connection at Lancaster for travellers from the West Riding to Scotland. The run-down of the fleet had commenced in 1981 and vehicles were withdrawn if they required heavy expenditure and 13th May 1984 the units made their final public appearance in passenger service. Unfortunately, the prohibitive cost of removing asbestos ruled out the chance of a 'Trans-Pennine' unit being preserved and all of the coaches went for scrap. *Tommy Tomalin*

On 1st January 1962 most services along the Calder Valley main line were turned over to DMU operation using a total of 30 sets constructed by the Birmingham Railway Carriage & Wagon Co. for use on this steeply graded route; ten were allocated to the LMR while the NER had 20 sets. Places served by this route included Liverpool and Manchester in the west and Harrogate plus York in the east, so some of the journey times were almost three hours long. The units (later Class 110) consisted of a Driving Motor Brake Composite coach (12 first class seats and 33 second), a Trailer Second Lavatory (72 second class seats) and a Driving Motor Composite Lavatory vehicle (12 first and 54 second class seats). The first class accommodation was located solely in motor coaches where passengers would have experienced much more noise and vibration than the trailer coach, but at least they had the compensation of a forward view through the cab windows. The units were powered by four 180hp Rolls Royce engines, two of which were fitted to each motor coach, so they had a very high power/weight ratio, this being necessary in view of the severe gradients on the route which included long climbs in each direction to Summit tunnel and some notoriously steep climbs between Bradford and Leeds. Four-character headcodes had been introduced by the time of their construction and the headcode box was fitted above the cab windows with two marker lights on the cab front panel. This stock had regular diagrams to and from Blackpool and this photograph shows one of these units forming a train to Leeds at Towneley, between Burnley and Todmorden (Hall Royd Junction), on 7th August 1968. Despite being regularly used by passenger trains this 'secret' line was, apparently, not considered sufficiently important to merit inclusion in the LMR timetable and if passengers looked out for clues regarding the train's location they would have been out of luck because there were no intermediate stations between those points. It is not known whether these trains were advertised as 'mystery tours' but this title certainly applied for part of the journey. There used to be a station at Towneley but it closed its doors from 4th August 1952. *Tommy Tomalin*

In June 1957 BR launched the first English Electric Type 1 locomotive into traffic, this being the first class to enter service as part of the modernisation programme. Later, North British, British Thomson-Houston and the Clayton Equipment Co. also produced their version of a Type 1 Bo-Bo locomotive but, unlike the English Electric machines, they were all utterly hopeless in service and BR top management probably wished they had remained loyal to English Electric. The first of the Clayton/Beyer Peacock locomotives appeared in September 1962 and was a marked breakaway from the usual design of Type 1 locomotives because it featured a centrally-placed cab with two engines mounted horizontally within low bonnets on either side. This design change was reportedly in response to complaints from some crews who were unhappy about the restricted vision available when working nose-leading on locomotives that had the cab located at one end. The 'Claytons' had two small six-cylinder Paxman 6ZHXL 450hp engines, weighed 68 tons and had four traction motors; it should be mentioned that Nos.D8586 and D8587 were an exception and had Rolls Royce engines. A total of 117 locomotives was built between late 1962 and April 1965. Despite the radical design of these locomotives there were still operating problems because crews could not see the area directly in front of the locomotive when shunting. The lion's share of these machines was based in Scotland, at Haymarket and Polmadie sheds, while examples were allocated to the North Eastern, London Midland and Eastern Regions. An unmitigated disaster, the availability of the class sunk as low as 60% and the first withdrawal took place in July 1968, just over three years after the last locomotive was delivered! Some other locomotives lasted less than five years in traffic. Meanwhile, production of the almost infallible English Electric Type 1s resumed in January 1966 with the final example being delivered in February 1968, just five months before the first 'Clayton' was taken out of service. What a contrast! Here, Nos.D8509 and D8523 are depicted at Carnforth on 5th June 1968, probably proceeding to the shed for attention. *Tommy Tomalin*

2nd-SINGLE SINGLE-2nd
3189 CHILD Hest Bank to CHILD 3189
Hest Bank / Lancaster (Castle) / or Carnforth
Hest Bank / Lancaster (Castle) / or Carnforth
LANCASTER (Castle) or CARNFORTH
(M) 0/5 Fare 0/5 (M)
For conditions see over For conditions see over

2nd-SINGLE SINGLE-2nd
7066 CHILD Bolton-le-Sands to CHILD 7066
Bolton-le-Sands / Carnforth
Bolton-le-Sands / Carnforth
CARNFORTH
(M) 0/3 Fare 0/3 (M)
For conditions see over For conditions see over

Going it alone. Some of the later 'Claytons' were allocated to Tinsley depot, Sheffield, and in this shot one of those, No.D8608, is seen with a southbound freight at Kirkby South Junction on 19th June 1965. The train is standing on the former Great Central Mansfield branch and is restarting following a signal check before joining the GC main line, the tracks of which are in the foreground. Interestingly, the Mansfield branch was very much a latecomer on the scene, not opening until the 1920s. Passenger services on this line did not last long, being withdrawn between Hollinwell & Annesley and Edwinstowe from 2nd January 1956, but it should be mentioned that the latter station continued to be served by seasonal trains until 5th September 1964. The life of the Mansfield branch may have been short but at least it lasted much longer than No.D8608 which was theoretically in service for only seven years. *Tommy Tomalin*

Safety in numbers? Judging by the fumes being emitted from the rear Clayton Type 1 locomotive, No.D8534, its engines were ticking over normally but the leading locomotive, No.D8500, appears to be rather lifeless. Cynics would probably contend that the latter had failed and Stanier Class 5MT 4-6-0 No.45134 was there to offer assistance if D8534 also 'conked out'. This picture was taken at Burton & Holme, just north of Carnforth, on 1st August 1968 during the last week of BR standard gauge steam traction and the Class 5MT's services would, sadly, not have been available much longer. The goods loops at this location were operated on the permissive block section principle which allowed for two trains at any one time.
The diesels were heading to Carnforth after working the 1.10pm Windermere to Kendal parcels train while the Black Five was on a local ballast turn. At least the 'Black Five', which entered service in May 1935, had a jolly good innings which is more than can be said for the hapless Clayton diesel locomotives. *Tommy Tomalin*

A young lad stares in disbelief at the row of withdrawn steam locomotives at Carnforth shed on 4th August 1968, no doubt regretting that he had been born too late to see anything worthwhile of the steam era. At least the locomotives seen here had been secured for preservation and the line included Fairburn Class 4MT 2-6-4T No.42073 and Ivatt Class 2MT 2-6-0 No.46441, nearest to the camera, plus a B1 Class 4-6-0 and BR Standard Class 4MT 4-6-0 No.75027 and other engines. But what of the ill-fated Clayton Type 1s on the adjoining track? The identities of the locomotives are unknown but it is likely they were out of service, the first example already having been withdrawn from traffic. Later in the year more were condemned, and by the end of 1968 a total of 32 locomotives had been withdrawn – rest in pieces. In the background Carnforth station's canopies can be seen together with rows of wagons and, of course, the massive coaling plant which is still standing at the time of writing. *Ron Herbert*

During the first years of BR's modernisation plan the only Type 4 diesel locomotives available were heavy 1Co-Co1 designs that were not particularly powerful in relation to their weight and BR was looking for a locomotive that was lighter and more powerful. Orders for a preliminary batch of 20 Brush Type 4 locomotives, were placed with the Brush Electrical Engineering works at Loughborough, this being part of the Hawker-Siddeley Group. The 2,750hp locomotives weighed only 114 tons (with variations), had six Brush traction motors and possessed a top speed of 95mph; their weight was considerably less than Type 4s already delivered. The Brush locomotives also had greater route availability compared to existing Type 4 designs. The external design and colour scheme were the result of collaboration with the British Transport Commission Design Panel, the livery consisting of BR standard green bodywork with a broad band of olive green along the middle of the bodysides. A total of 512 locomotives was eventually constructed between September 1962 and January 1968, 310 by Brush at Loughborough with the remainder being built by BR at Crewe. It should be noted that in the early 1970s BR decided to de-rate the class's power output to 2,580hp to minimise stress on the power plant and improve availability. The class was initially known as the Hawker-Siddeley Type 4 but later the description Brush Type 4 was generally in common use. The locomotives were nothing if not versatile and could be observed across Great Britain on virtually any type of working from express passenger to slow-moving goods workings and some examples were built without any train heating solely for freight working. In this picture, taken at Low Gill on 30th April 1966, No.D1845 is seen hauling a southbound goods train; unfortunately its attractive two-tone green livery has been lost under a liberal coating of grime. The train is passing the site of the former Low Gill station, closed from 7th March 1960, and the tracks on the right are those of the erstwhile branch to Ingleton. *Tommy Tomalin*

A southbound coal train, headed by Brush Type 4 No.D1517, was photographed south of the former Harringworth station, between Melton Mowbray and Kettering, on 24th April 1968; the site of the station, which lost its passenger service from 1st November 1948, is just visible in the far distance. No.D1517 was one of the first series of these locomotives to be constructed and it began its career in April 1963 at Finsbury Park depot for service on the East Coast Main Line. *Tommy Tomalin*

Photographed south of Kelmarsh, on the now lifted Market Harborough to Northampton line, No.D1578 is seen with a coal train on 30th May 1968. The appealing two-tone green colours applied to these locomotives certainly looked fine when they were clean but these intensively used locomotives soon became dirty with the rigours of everyday use, as seen here. *Tommy Tomalin*

Another shot taken on the Market Harborough to Northampton line. Photographs of sleeping car trains are not plentiful for obvious reasons but here is a picture of No.D1627 powering the 10.50pm (previous night) Glasgow Central to London Euston train in the wilds of Northamptonshire on 29th May 1969; the shot was taken just north of Brixworth. The train had clearly been diverted from its normal route along the West Coast Main Line, and was presumably running to a revised schedule, but at least it was on time when it passed the photographer at 7.58am. Regular travellers must have thought their train had got lost or perhaps they were resigned to Sunday diversions along strange routes. *Tommy Tomalin*

The Settle & Carlisle line boasts some of the finest railway photographic locations in Great Britain and this spot, surely, is one of the best, looking down Dentdale with the majestic Dent Head viaduct in the foreground. The course of the line, running along a ledge cut into the fell side, can be discerned. In this illustration an unidentified Class 47 rushes across the viaduct with a diverted West Coast Main Line express on 6th May 1982. The viaduct is one of this line's many iconic structures, 177 yards long, 100 feet above the valley floor, and has a strengthening centre pier. Constructed between 1870 and 1875 of blue limestone with brick arch rings, the ten openings are a nominal 45 feet wide. In the distance can be seen Rise Hill, 1,825 feet above sea level, while in the far distance beyond it is Baugh Fell which rises to 2,216 feet. *Tommy Tomalin*

Saturday 2nd April 1983 was a day of intense activity on the Settle & Carlisle line (as previously mentioned) as a result of the WCML being closed due to bridge replacement work at Tebay and the extra workings attracted many observers to the lineside; the weather was as unpredictable as ever ranging from warm spring sunshine to a raging blizzard. The 'action' did not really start until mid-morning which gave the author plenty of time to cycle (yes, really!) from Sedburgh to Dent station, arriving just in time to photograph the 8.57am Leeds to Carlisle passing through behind Class 31 No.31 404. In this photograph the 8.10am Birmingham New Street to Glasgow Central, with No.47 541 *The Queen Mother* in charge, is surrounded by bare moorland as it approaches the southern entrance to Rise Hill tunnel, between Dent and Garsdale, in the morning sunshine. *Author*

Most of the largest bridges and viaducts on the North Wales coast main line are well known but the distinctive viaduct at Bodorgan, that takes the line across the Afon Cefni, does not have such a high profile, perhaps due to its more remote location on Anglesey. One would have thought that an embankment would have been adequate at this spot but perhaps this area, which is less than a mile from the sea, is prone to flooding and this was a factor in the decision to construct a viaduct when the line was built. Here, No.47 465 is depicted dashing across with an express for Holyhead on 30th August 1983. *Tommy Tomalin*

The steep decline in the fortunes of the railway industry throughout the 1960s started to be reversed in the '70s and the opening of Alfreton & Mansfield Parkway station on 7th May 1973 was a manifestation of this change of direction. The new station was, as its name suggests, designed to serve the nearby towns of Alfreton and Mansfield both of which had lost their passenger services as a result of the Beeching axe, the latter being one of the largest towns in Great Britain without a rail passenger service. When the Nottingham to Worksop line, which had served Mansfield, was closed in 1964 most of the infrastructure was retained for goods traffic and it was later reopened, but did not provide direct trains to London, unlike 'Parkway' station. One of the advantages of the new station from the motorist's point of view is the huge car park, part of which is seen on the left in this picture of No.47 353 running-in with the 1.00pm Sheffield to St. Pancras train on 20th July 1974; judging by the heavy luggage some passengers were evidently just setting off on their holidays. No.47 353 was one of a number of these machines built without any form of train heating solely for use on freight work, but it would have been able to work passenger trains during the summer period, as seen here. Note that it is still sporting two-tone green livery, almost ten years after the introduction of corporate blue. The station originally on this site, known as 'Alfreton & South Normanton', was closed from 2nd January 1967 as part of the withdrawal of services from all local stations between Sheffield and Nottingham via Pye Bridge. *Chris Evans*

The Settle & Carlisle line has been variously described as inhospitable, desolate and remote and in the depths of winter the dreadful weather conditions deter all but the bravest (or most foolhardy?) adventurer. Here, an unidentified Class 47 is apparently making good headway through Dentdale with a diverted WCML express and the passengers are, hopefully, nice and cosy in their air conditioned carriages while the photographer wonders whether the nearby Sportsman Inn is open on Sunday afternoons, thus enabling him to 'defrost'. This picture was taken in the spring of 1984 but the bitter conditions suggest that spring was late in coming to Dentdale. *Author*

Judging by the menacing dark clouds in the distance a storm is imminent as the 6.15pm Llandudno to Stoke-on-Trent train, powered by No. 47 609 *Firefly,* leaves Abergele on 14th August 1986; presumably this was a summer only 'bucket and spade' working for day trippers. This locomotive was built at Crewe works as No.D1656 and entered traffic in February 1965; when the TOPS numbering scheme was introduced it became No.47 072. A further change of identity occurred in April 1984 when it was re-numbered 47 609 following the fitting of electric train heating equipment. In July 1989 No.47 609 was fitted with long-range fuel tanks and became No.47 834. In 1995 it was renumbered 47 798 and renamed *Prince William* for Royal train duties so it has carried five different numbers; at the time of writing it is based at the National Railway Museum and has main line certification. *Chris Evans*

More dark clouds at Abergele. The class 47 locomotives were truly maids of all work and could be found on a wide variety of duties and in this picture No.47 364 is seen heading westwards towards Holyhead with a Freightliner working; this shot was taken on 15th August 1986. Some of the smaller intermediate stations between Chester and Holyhead suffered piecemeal closures over a long period, Llysfaen, near Colwyn Bay, closing as long ago as 5th January 1931, while nearby Llandulas closed its doors from 1st December 1952. Many of the remaining wayside stations were scheduled for closure in the Beeching Report and lost their passenger services from 14th February 1966. *Chris Evans*

The later Swindon 'Inter City' units (known as Class 123) were the last new design of first generation DMUs to enter traffic. They were combined with 'Trans Pennine' units for use on the Manchester to Cleethorpes service and other routes in the north of England. Originally introduced on the Western Region in 1963 for the Swansea to Derby via Birmingham route, and other lines radiating from Bristol/Cardiff, the stylish 'Inter City' units were the last word in luxury compared to many of their predecessors, being based on the Mk.1 coach design and fitted with B4/B5 bogies for a smooth ride and were particularly well insulated from noise and draughts. The seating was very comfortable and based on ergonomic principles, all saloons and compartments had curtains while mirrors were fitted to many bulkheads. Externally, they had gangwayed front ends with wrap-around windscreens which gave them a very distinctive appearance. Ten 4-car units were built, five of which incorporated a buffet car, and passenger accommodation was provided in a mix of open and compartment vehicles; the units were powered by 230hp Leyland Albion engines. The original formations were DMBS/TCK/TS/DMSK but it should be noted that five units had a TSRB coach in place of a TS carriage; these buffet vehicles were withdrawn in 1970, however, thus reducing some units to three cars only. Despite their status as the most opulent DMUs constructed, apart from the Pullman units, they never really found a permanent home and were moved between depots on the WR until being declared redundant in 1977 because the region had no further use for them, and the units went into store. The ER's Chief Passenger Manager then stepped in, seeing an opportunity to improve the level of service on the 'South Trans-Pennine' Manchester to Cleethorpes and Hull routes via Sheffield, and the first three cars arrived at Hull Botanic Gardens depot on 5th June 1977 to start a 'new life', so to speak, combined with the existing 'Trans Pennine' units (later Class 124); these units also worked various services radiating from Leeds. BR planned to introduce a new, loco-hauled service using Class 31s on the 'South Trans-Pennine' route in May 1984 and the run-down of the DMU fleet at Botanic Gardens started only a few years after the arrival of the Class 123 units, the final duties being on 13th May 1984; it is likely that the cost of removing blue asbestos may have been a factor in their demise. In this picture, taken at a wintry Grindleford on 24th February 1979, the 9.45am Manchester Piccadilly to Sheffield train is seen passing through the station. The vehicle nearest to the camera is a DMBS which was formed of two 16-seat saloons and was fitted with a curved top fibreglass gangway shield. These units were not equipped with marker lights, consequently guards had to ensure a tail lamp was displayed at the rear of the train; presumably red roller blinds were fitted but WR signalmen were instructed not to accept that indication of the rear of a train, hence the anachronistic tail lamps were mandatory. *Tommy Tomalin*

A train bound for Manchester, with a DMBS vehicle leading, is seen leaving Romiley in April 1984, shortly before the demise of these distinctive former 'Inter City' units. The original character of the unit's front end has been changed considerably, the train classification boxes having been replaced; in addition the communicating door on this coach appears to have been sealed out of use. There were variations regarding the extent of the grey livery, some vehicles were painted blue and grey up to and including the cab door, as seen here, while on others the door was entirely rail blue. Bearing in mind that these units represented the zenith of first generation DMU design it is to be regretted that no coaches passed into preservation, the cost of removing blue asbestos contamination no doubt being the deciding factor. *Author*

In the mid-1960s BR was looking for a new Type 4 Co-Co locomotive with a 100mph capability and decided that a new design based on the English Electric prototype No.DP2 was ideal for its needs. This machine had entered service in May 1962 and employed an English Electric 16 cylinder 16CSVT engine which developed 2,700hp and powered six traction motors. Unfortunately, this locomotive met an untimely end when it ran into a derailed cement train at Thirsk in July 1967 and was damaged beyond repair. The first of the production series locomotives, No.D400, emerged from the Vulcan Foundry works at Newton-le-Willows in August 1967 and 50 machines were constructed, the last entering traffic in December 1968. Most unusually, the entire class was leased from the manufacturer for ten years and then BR purchased it outright. BR was anxious to speed up services to Scotland on the West Coast Main Line and the class was put to work mainly on Anglo-Scottish trains north of Crewe which at that time had only recently been authorised for electrification. The new timetable introduced in May 1970 featured greatly accelerated services employing double-headed English Electric 2,700hp Type 4 locomotives. The Class 50s, as they later became known, were plagued by reliability problems, their Achilles heel being main generator failures caused by deficiencies in the air filtration system. When the Crewe to Glasgow line was fully electrified in 1974 the Class 50s moved to the Western Region where they helped displace that region's fleet of diesel hydraulic locomotives. Between 1979 and 1983 the class underwent a refurbishment programme at Doncaster works which was only partially successful in curing the class's problems and the first withdrawals occurred in 1987. The final commemorative rail tours took place in March 1994 when enthusiasts said 'farewell' to this popular class which, arguably, was the least successful of English Electric's otherwise excellent stud of locomotives used on BR tracks. Here, No.D407 is seen at Morecambe South Junction with an up train on 5th June 1968. *Tommy Tomalin*

The 4.10pm Windermere to London Euston train is seen at Burneside, between Windermere and Kendal, on 10th June 1968; motive power is provided by No.D404. In the 1967/68 timetable this train was booked to leave Windermere at 4.08pm and arrive in Euston at 9.01pm so it was not a particularly speedy journey; ten minutes were allowed at Crewe to change engines from diesel to electric. No.D404 entered traffic in December 1967 and was named *St. Vincent* in May 1978 by which time it had been re-allocated to the WR; it was taken out of service in June 1990. *Tommy Tomalin*

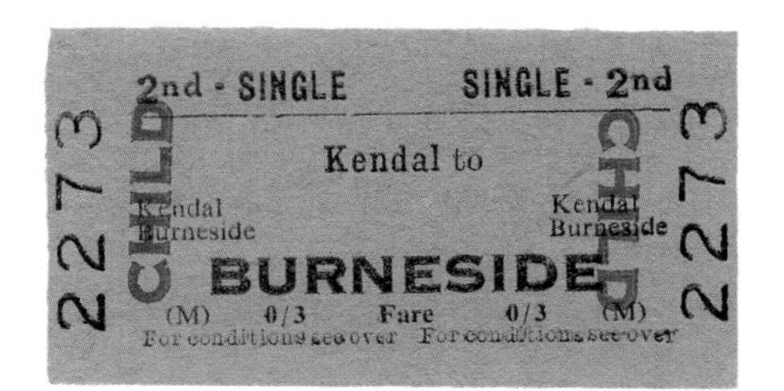
2nd - SINGLE SINGLE - 2nd
2273 CHILD Kendal to CHILD 2273
Kendal Burneside Kendal Burneside
BURNESIDE
(M) 0/3 Fare 0/3 (M)
For conditions see over For conditions see over

During their sojourn on the West Coast Main Line the English Electric 2,700hp Type 4s were employed, as might be expected, on miscellaneous duties in addition to their principal tasks of hauling the fast Anglo-Scottish expresses. In this picture No.D408 is depicted heading southwards at Scout Green on 29th August 1969 with a short parcels working – clearly not the type of exacting work on passenger trains the class was designed to perform. No.D408 was later bestowed with the name *Thunderer* and upon withdrawal became one of no fewer than 18 members of the class to enter preservation and, at the time of writing, can be seen at the East Lancashire Railway. *Richard Lewis/Rail Photoprints*

Two heads are better than one. The 'D400s' were not, as previously mentioned, the most reliable of locomotives and were known in some enthusiast circles as the '50/50s' which, presumably, referred to the possibility of reaching one's destination on time or, indeed, at all. The London Midland Region's May 1970 timetable featured quite dramatic acceleration of Anglo-Scottish trains following the decision to double-head those trains on the non-electrified section north of Crewe. The down 'Royal Scot', for example, left Euston at 10.05am and in the 1967/68 timetable was due in Glasgow Central at 4.45pm with stops at Crewe and Carlisle only. In the 1970/71 timetable its departure time from London was unchanged but arrival in Glasgow was at 3.59pm, again after two intermediate stops. Here, Nos. D448 and D421 are depicted at Galgate, just south of Lancaster, in May 1971. The buildings of Lancaster University can just be seen on the extreme right of the picture. The lady responsible for the typesetting and production of this album, Lucy Frontani, was particularly pleased to see this shot included – she was a student there in the late 1990s. *Rail Photoprints collection*

A scene at Crewe on 20th October 1972 with No.411 entering the station with a London-bound express. Interestingly, this train was actually made up of two portions, one from Carlisle and another from Blackpool, which had presumably been combined at Preston. In years gone by multi-portion trains to and from London were commonplace on the WCML and enabled many destinations to be served that would not have justified a train of their own. Locations such as Barrow-in-Furness, Southport and Windermere were served directly from London at one time but, presumably, BR found it inconvenient to run through services as this involved long waits at stations as attachments/detachments were made for the benefit of a relatively small number of passengers. No.411 was later christened *Centurion* but its main claim to fame was the fact that it became the first Class 50 to be condemned, in February 1987. *Terry Phillips*